my **revisi⏻n** notes

A2 OCR History
REBELLION AND DISORDER UNDER THE TUDORS
1485–1603

Nicholas Fellows

HODDER
EDUCATION
AN HACHETTE UK COMPANY

Thanks are due to OCR for permission to reproduce the mark scheme on page 3. This is from OCR GCE History A unit F966: Historical Themes, Option A: Medieval and Early Modern 1066–1715, 2007.

Every effort has been made to trace all copyright holders, but if any have been inadvertently overlooked the Publishers will be pleased to make the necessary arrangements at the first opportunity.

Hachette UK's policy is to use papers that are natural, renewable and recyclable products and made from wood grown in sustainable forests. The logging and manufacturing processes are expected to conform to the environmental regulations of the country of origin.

Orders: please contact Bookpoint Ltd, 130 Milton Park, Abingdon, Oxon OX14 4SB. Telephone: +44 (0)1235 827720. Fax: +44 (0)1235 400454. Lines are open 9.00a.m.–5.00p.m., Monday to Saturday, with a 24-hour message answering service. Visit our website at www.hoddereducation.co.uk.

© Nicholas Fellows 2014
First published in 2014 by
Hodder Education,
an Hachette UK company
338 Euston Road
London NW1 3BH
Impression number 10 9 8 7 6 5 4 3 2 1
Year 2018 2017 2016 2015 2014

Typeset in 11/13 Stempel Schneidler Std-Light by Datapage (India) Pvt. Ltd.
Printed and bound in India

A catalogue record for this title is available from the British Library
ISBN 978 1 444 199673

Contents

Introduction

About Unit F966/01

Unit F966/01 is worth 30 per cent of your A level. It requires that you are able to:

- recall, select and deploy historical knowledge appropriately, and communicate knowledge and understanding of history in a clear and effective manner
- demonstrate an understanding of the past through explanation and analysis
- make judgements about key concepts (change/continuity; similarity/difference; cause/consequence).

Most important is that you will be expected to view the theme synoptically. In other words, you should look to make links between events over the whole period and, where appropriate, with other topics that you have studied during your History course. In turn, a synoptic approach demands that you write essays using the skill of synthesis. You will need to be able to compare and contrast developments over a long period of time and make judgements based on your observations. Factual knowledge will be used to support your judgements about the main developments and turning points relevant to the theme. Acquisition of detailed factual knowledge is a secondary requirement to the ability to think synoptically and to write with synthesis.

In the examination you will be required to answer two questions from three on the theme you have been taught. The examination lasts for two hours unless you have been awarded extra time. Each essay question is worth 60 marks and you should therefore spend an hour answering each question. However, it is **very** important that you spend a reasonable amount of time planning your responses (5–10 minutes for each essay). Effective planning will enable you to produce a genuinely synoptic answer.

Exam tip

Avoid answering questions using a narrative, chronological and descriptive approach. This will almost definitely confine your responses to Level IV and below.

Rebellion and disorder under the Tudors 1485–1603

The awarding body specifies that for this topic you need to study the following:

1 **The main causes of rebellion and disorder:** political factions, the succession, religion, taxation, famine, inflation, enclosures and social issues.

2 **The frequency and nature of disturbances:** regional variations, objectives, size, support, leadership, organisation, differences between rebellions in England and Ireland; reasons for the limited success and/or failure of rebellions.

3 **The impact of disturbances upon Tudor governments:** their response to the threat of disorder at the time and subsequently (changes in government strategy, policies, legislation, propaganda); the extent to which rebellions presented a serious threat to the government.

4 **The maintenance of political stability:** the role of local and central authorities, especially the Crown, the Church, nobility, gentry, lieutenants, sheriffs, JPs; popular attitudes towards authority.

The awarding body also makes clear that the theme 'focuses on the nature and extent of rebellion and disorder in England and Ireland during this period. The following revolts and rebellions should be studied: Lovel, Simnel, Yorkshire, Warbeck, Cornish, Amicable Grant, Kildare, Pilgrimage of Grace, Western, Kett, Northumberland, Wyatt, Shane O'Neill, Northern Earls, Fitzgerald, Geraldine, Tyrone O'Neill, Oxfordshire and Essex.'

How to use this book

This book has been designed to help you develop the knowledge and skills necessary to succeed in the examination. The book is divided into five sections. The first four sections cover each general area of the course and are made up of a series of topics organised into double-page spreads. On the left-hand page, you will find a summary of the key content you will need to learn. Words in bold in the key content are defined in the glossary (pages 86–88). On the right-hand page, you will find exam-focused activities. Together, these two strands of the book will take you through the knowledge and skills essential for exam success.

There are three levels of exam-focused activities:

- Band 1 activities are designed to develop the foundational skills needed to pass the exam. These have a turquoise heading and this symbol:

- Band 2 activities are designed to build on the skills developed in Band 1 activities and to help you achieve a C grade. These have an orange heading and this symbol:

- Band 3 activities are designed to enable you to access the highest grades. These have a purple heading and this symbol:

Some of the activities have answers or suggested answers on pages 90–94 and have the following symbol to indicate this:

Others are intended for you to complete in pairs and assess by comparing answers. These do not have answers given at the back of the book.

The fifth section in the book provides exam-style questions and model A grade answer with commentary. This should give you guidance on what is required to achieve the top grades.

You can also keep track of your revision by ticking off each topic heading in the book, or by ticking the checklist on the contents page. Tick each box when you have:

- revised and understood a topic
- completed the activities.

Mark scheme

For some of the activities in the book it will be useful to refer to the mark scheme for the unit. Remember that the book is devised to help you achieve high grades. The activities push you to progress to write at Level II or above. Hence, below is the mark scheme for Unit F966/01 showing just the first two levels (and not levels III to VII).

AOs	AO1a	AO1b
Total mark for each question = 60	Recall, select and deploy historical knowledge appropriately, and communicate knowledge and understanding of history in a clear and effective manner	Demonstrate understanding of the past through explanation, analysis and arriving at substantiated judgements of: • key concepts such as causation, consequence, continuity, change and significance within an historical context • The relationships between key features and characteristics of the periods studied
Level IA	• Uses a wide range of accurate and relevant evidence • Accurate and confident use of appropriate historical terminology • Answer is clearly structured and coherent; communicates accurately and legibly 18–20	• Excellent understanding of key concepts (e.g. continuity and change) relevant to analysis in their historical context • Excellent synthesis and synoptic assessment • Answer is consistently and relevantly analytical with developed explanations and supported judgements • May make unexpected but substantiated connections over the whole period 36–40
Level IB	• Uses accurate and relevant evidence • Accurate use of a range of appropriate historical terminology • Answer is clearly structured and mostly coherent; communicates accurately and legibly 16–17	• Very good level of understanding of key concepts (e.g. continuity and change) in their historical context • Answer is consistently focused on the question set • Very good level of explanation/analysis, and provides supported judgements • Very good synthesis and synoptic assessment of the whole period 32–35
Level II	• Uses mostly accurate and relevant evidence • Generally accurate use of historical terminology • Answer is structured and mostly coherent; writing is legible and communication is generally clear 14–15	• Good level of understanding of key concepts (e.g. continuity and change) in their historical context • Good explanation/analysis but overall judgements may be uneven • Answer is focused on the issues in the question set • Good synthesis and assessment of developments over most of the period 28–31

Rebellion and disorder under the Tudors: an overview

There were a large number of rebellions throughout the Tudor period and every Tudor monarch faced challenges from some of their subjects. However, most of the population obeyed the demands of the state. Over the whole Tudor period probably no more than 80,000 Englishmen actively rebelled, from a total population of some 15 million.

Regardless of the question you are answering, you will need to know details of the main rebellions in both England and Ireland and use them as examples of the causes and nature of rebellions and the government's response to them as it attempted to maintain stability. The main rebellions are outlined on these two pages.

Henry VII (1485–1509)

Henry VII, a Lancastrian, faced five major challenges to his throne. He had won the crown in 1485 at the Battle of Bosworth, but the defeated **Yorkist** family launched a number of rebellions to try and regain the throne.

Lovel and Stafford Rebellion (1486)

The first came within a year of Henry's accession with the Lovel and Stafford Rebellion in 1486. Francis Viscount Lovel and Humphrey Stafford, councillors to Richard III and Yorkists, had avoided capture at the Battle of Bosworth, took sanctuary at Colchester and escaped and raised troops in an attempt to overthrow Henry. The rebellion failed, Lovel fled to Flanders and Stafford was executed.

Simnel Rebellion (1486–87)

Soon after this, in 1486–87, Henry faced the Simnel Rebellion. Lambert Simnel claimed to be the Yorkist Earl of Warwick, who had a better claim to the throne than Henry as the son of the Duke of Clarence and cousin to Edward V. Although he had some English and Irish noble support he was defeated at the Battle of East Stoke.

Yorkshire (1489) and Cornish (1497) Rebellions

The next two rebellions were over taxation. First, Yorkshire rebelled in 1489 over funding a war in France. The rebels killed the Earl of Northumberland, who had been sent to collect the tax, before being defeated. Then, in 1497, Cornwall rebelled over taxes to fight the Scots. Although the Cornish rebels marched to London, they were slaughtered at Blackheath, the leaders were executed and the county was fined.

Warbeck's Rebellion (1491–99)

Perkin Warbeck's rebellion lasted from 1491 until 1499. He claimed to be Richard, Duke of York – one of the **Princes in the Tower**. He won support from some nobles and, at times, from foreign powers. However, his attempted invasion in 1497 ended in defeat in the West Country. He was captured and executed in 1499.

Henry VIII (1509–47)

Although seen as the most powerful Tudor monarch, Henry faced three rebellions, two of which were large scale.

The Amicable Grant Rising (1525)

The Amicable Grant Rising in 1525 was a response to the heavy tax demands to fund the war in France. The scale of the rising, which involved large numbers of peasants and had some noble sympathy, engulfed much of East Anglia and parts of the Home Counties and Midlands, and forced the government to abandon the tax.

The Silken Thomas Rebellion (1534–37)

The Silken Thomas Rebellion was an Irish rebellion that followed the arrest and imprisonment of the father of Thomas O'Neill (also known as **Silken Thomas**), the Earl of Kildare. The Kildare family had acted as the Crown's deputy in Ireland, but had begun to be replaced by English officials. The rebels were defeated and executed.

The Pilgrimage of Grace (1536–37)

Three separate risings in the north of England in 1536–37, usually referred to as the Pilgrimage of Grace, were a reaction to the religious changes of the **Reformation**, as well as underlying social and economic grievances. The rebel force numbered some 40,000 at its height and Henry was forced to 'play for time' by negotiating with the rebels, before going back on his promises and executing over 200 rebels.

Edward VI (1547–53)

Two large-scale rebellions and a series of smaller risings have led to 1549 being known as the 'commotion time'.

The Western Rebellion (1549)

The Western rebels besieged Exeter and wanted an end to the Protestant reforms, as well as an end to taxes on sheep and wool. It took the government five battles to finally defeat them at the battle of Clyst Heath.

Kett's Rebellion (1549)

Kett's Rebellion in Norfolk was largely social and economic. The rebels established a series of camps, even captured Norwich, and were only defeated at the Battle of Dussindale.

Smaller riots

Meanwhile, most of central and southern England witnessed smaller scale risings, often about social and economic grievances, which the local **gentry** and nobility were able to control.

Mary Tudor (1553–58)

Although Mary faced a challenge from Lady Jane Grey before she was able to take the throne, she faced only one other rebellion during her reign, despite the supposed unpopularity of her religious policy and the burning of many Protestants.

Lady Jane Grey (1553)

Mary's accession to the throne was initially successfully challenged by the **Lord President of the Council**, the Duke of Northumberland. He succeeded in having his daughter-in-law Lady Jane Grey crowned. She was the great niece of Henry VIII and granddaughter of his sister Mary, making her the next in line to the throne if Mary Tudor and Elizabeth were excluded. However, Mary Tudor raised a force and Northumberland submitted without a fight after nine days. Lady Jane Grey was executed.

Wyatt's Rebellion (1554)

The second challenge to Mary came from Thomas Wyatt in Kent. It was initially planned as a four-pronged attack on London to prevent Mary's marriage to Philip of Spain. The rebels feared England would be dominated by Spaniards and there would be a re-establishment of a Catholic dynasty. Wyatt was the only rebel who was able to raise troops (he raised 5000 men) and reached Ludgate (London), where he was finally arrested and later executed.

Elizabeth I (1558–1603)

Although the number of rebellions in England declined dramatically in the second half of the Tudor period, with Elizabeth facing only three rebellions in over 40 years, the situation in Ireland was very different.

Irish rebellions

- Shane O'Neill rose in 1558, resentful at losing the earldom of Tyrone to his brother. The rebellion ended only in 1567 when he was killed in inter-clan fighting.

- The Fitzgerald or Munster Rebellion (1569–73) was in response to English **plantations** in Munster. It started as a private war between the Earls of Desmond and Ormonde, but Desmond's cousin appealed for foreign help and this worried Elizabeth. Although this unrest was quickly put down, it led to further unrest against the plantations. Fitzgerald fled to Rome, but he returned to lead a second rebellion (the Geraldine) in 1579. This time the protests were about increased English control and the imposition of religious reform. Although Fitzgerald was killed, his brother succeeded him as Earl of Desmond and took over the rebellion until defeated and executed in 1583.

- The final Irish rebellion, led by Hugh O'Neill, Earl of Tyrone, lasted from 1595 to 1603. This large-scale rising saw much of Ireland in arms against English rule and there were several English defeats, for example at Yellow Ford in 1598. It was only when Elizabeth sent sufficient forces, under Lord Mountjoy, that the rebellion was crushed.

English rebellions

- The most serious English rebellion, with 5000 men, was that of the Northern Earls in 1569. Northumberland and Westmorland planned to marry Mary Queen of Scots to the Duke of Norfolk and force Elizabeth to name her as heir to the throne. However, the rebellion got little support and most rebels fled as the royal army approached. Northumberland was executed, but Westmorland was not caught.

- The Oxfordshire Rising of 1596 over **enclosure** is best remembered for its abject failure. Only four rebels turned up, but this did not prevent the government from executing all of them.

- The final challenge to Elizabeth came from a courtier and former favourite, the Earl of Essex. His attempt in 1601 to raise London against the dominance of the **Cecil faction** lasted only twelve hours. Essex was captured and executed.

Section 1: The main causes of rebellion and disorder

Dynastic succession 1

For a description of all the rebellions mentioned see pages 4–5.

As a result of the Yorkist defeat at the Battle of Bosworth and the replacement of the Yorkists by the Tudors, dynastic unrest was a major cause of rebellion at the start of the period as the Yorkists sought to remove Henry VII. The desire to overthrow the Tudors or change the succession remained a main or contributing cause to many of the rebellions throughout the period 1485–1603. The three main reasons for rebellion at this time were:

- revenge
- ambition
- principle.

Henry VII (1485–1509)

Henry VII's reign saw the most frequent and serious dynastic challenges because his claim to the throne was weak. He had won the throne on the battlefield and was a **usurper**. Although he had killed Richard III, there were remaining **Yorkists** with a stronger claim to the throne than him. Three of the rebellions he faced were mainly caused by the issue of dynastic succession.

Lovel and Stafford (1486)

Viscount Lovel, one of Richard III's former councillors, and the Yorkists Humphrey and Thomas Stafford raised troops to kill Henry as he travelled to his northern capital. Henry's spies warned him and an armed force was sent to deal with the rebels, who wanted to replace Henry with a leading Yorkist, either the Earl of Warwick or de la Pole. The rebels dispersed; Lovel fled to Flanders and the Staffords sought sanctuary from the Church. Nevertheless, Henry arrested the Staffords and executed one and pardoned the other.

Lambert Simnel, 1487

Richard Symonds, a priest from Oxford, claimed that Lambert Simnel, one of his pupils, was the Earl of Warwick. Warwick was Richard III's nephew, whom Henry had imprisoned in the Tower of London. The conspiracy was supported by a number of people, including:

- the Earl of Lincoln, Richard III's nephew whom Richard had named as his heir
- Viscount Lovel
- Margaret of Burgundy, Edward IV's sister
- the Irish Earl of Kildare.

They gathered together a force of over 2000 **mercenaries** in Ireland, paid for by Margaret. Although Henry paraded the real Earl to show Simnel was an impostor, it did not stop the rising. The rebel army landed in Lancashire, but failed to raise much support. Henry's forces met them at Stoke. It took Henry's army three hours to win. The battle showed that the fate of the monarchy could still be decided by battle and Henry, aware of his weak position, married Elizabeth of York to try and unite the two houses.

Warbeck's Rebellion (1491–99)

Perkin Warbeck pretended to be the Duke of York, another of Richard III's nephews, who had probably been murdered by Richard when he had seized the throne. Despite this ridiculous claim, he still raised foreign support from France, Burgundy and Scotland. However, Henry's foreign policy of making alliances with countries that offered Warbeck a base meant that attempts to launch an attack were unsuccessful until 1497:

- 1495 – Attempted landing at Deal but lack of support forced him to flee to Ireland.
- 1495 – Failed to take Waterford in Ireland and departed for Scotland.
- 1496 – Attempted invasion from Scotland, a disaster.
- 1497 – Departed for Ireland, gained little support.
- 1497 – Sailed for south-west England, driven out of Exeter and Taunton.
- 1497 – Fled to sanctuary, but persuaded to give himself up.

Spectrum of significance

Below is a sample exam question and a list of general points which could be used to answer the question. Use your own knowledge and the information on the opposite page and page 8 to reach a judgement about the importance of these general points to the question posed. Write the numbers on the spectrum below to indicate their relative importance. Having done this, write a brief justification of your placement, explaining why some of these factors are more important than others. The resulting diagram could form the basis of an essay plan.

'The most important cause of dynastic unrest was the Yorkist desire for revenge.' How far do you agree?

1 The Yorkists' stronger claim to the throne
2 The Yorkist desire for revenge after the death of Richard III
3 The ambition of Margaret of Burgundy
4 The ambition of the Duke of Northumberland
5 Factional disputes
6 The principle of legitimacy

←————————————————————————————→

Most important   Least important

 Develop the detail

Below is a sample exam question and a paragraph written in answer to this question. The paragraph contains a limited amount of detail. Using the information from the opposite page and from page 8 annotate the paragraph to add additional detail to the answer.

To what extent were dynastic rebellions a cause of unrest throughout the period?

Dynastic rebellions were a cause of unrest throughout the period to a limited extent. This was because the Tudor regime became more secure as the period progressed. There was a lot of dynastic unrest at the start of the period. The reign of Henry VII saw the most dynastic unrest as there were attempts to remove the Tudors, but there was also dynastic unrest under the later Tudor rulers, although the challenge was not as serious. There were also attempts to alter the succession, although not necessarily to remove the Tudors.

Dynastic succession 2

For a description of all the rebellions mentioned see pages 4–5.

Henry VIII: The Pilgrimage of Grace (1536–37)

Although not a main cause of unrest, as part of the Pilgrimage of Grace rebellion (see page 4) the rebels demanded that Henry's daughter Mary was restored to the succession, having been declared illegitimate following Henry's divorce from Catherine of Aragon.

Mary Tudor (1553–58)

Lady Jane Grey (1553)

The **Devise** of the dying Edward VI aimed to exclude Mary Tudor from the throne in favour of Lady Jane Grey, who was the daughter-in-law of the Duke of Northumberland, the **Lord President of the Council**. This was initially successful and Jane was crowned. However, Mary was able to rally support and Northumberland surrendered after nine days.

Wyatt's Rebellion (1554)

Thomas Wyatt, a courtier under both Henry VIII and Edward VI and member of the Kentish gentry, wanted to ensure the succession of Mary's sister, Elizabeth. For this reason he wanted to prevent Mary from marrying Philip of Spain, as any children born to the couple would prevent Elizabeth's succession. The rebels denied they wanted to overthrow Mary. Having raised a force in Kent and marched to London they were finally stopped at the gates of the city.

Elizabeth I (1558–1603)

The Northern Earls (1569)

The Northern Earls rebelled in order to ensure Mary Queen of Scots' position as the legitimate heir to the throne should Elizabeth die childless. They wanted Mary to marry the Duke of Norfolk and Elizabeth to name her as heir to the throne, thus guaranteeing a Catholic succession. It is unclear whether the rebels wanted to remove Elizabeth and replace her with Mary.

The Earl of Essex (1601)

The Earl of Essex claimed he did not want to harm Elizabeth, but wanted to endear himself to the likely heir, James VI of Scotland, by forcing her to acknowledge James as the legitimate heir. Essex wanted Elizabeth to remove her present councillors and replace them with himself and his supporters, making him the 'kingmaker'.

Support or challenge?

Below is a sample exam question which asks how far you agree with a specific statement. Below this are a series of general statements which are relevant to the question. Using your own knowledge of the whole period and the information on the opposite page and page 6 decide whether these statements support or challenge the statement in the question and tick the appropriate box.

'Dynastic challenges to the Tudors were not a serious cause of unrest in the period 1485 to 1603.'
How far do you agree with this statement?

	SUPPORT	CHALLENGE
The defeat of Richard III at Bosworth did not end the Yorkist threat.		
The Lovel and Stafford Rebellion occurred within one year of Henry VII acceding to the throne.		
Henry's victory at East Stoke against Simnel was the last battle a Tudor monarch faced.		
Warbeck's Rebellion was more a nuisance than a threat to Henry VII.		
The Pilgrims wanted to restore Mary to the succession.		
Lady Jane Grey was crowned queen.		
Wyatt wanted to ensure Elizabeth's succession.		
The Northern Earls wanted the Duke of Norfolk to marry Mary Queen of Scots.		
Essex wanted to win favour with James VI.		

Turning assertion into argument (a)

Below is a sample question and a series of assertions. Read the exam question and then add a justification to each of the assertions to turn each one into an argument.

'Dynastic factors were the most important cause of unrest in the period from 1485 to 1603.' How far do you agree with this view?

Dynastic problems were a major cause of unrest during the reign of Henry VII because

_____

_____

However, their importance declined as the period progressed because

_____

_____

Although dynastic issues were still a cause of unrest in Elizabeth I's reign as

_____

_____

_____

Taxation

> For a description of all the rebellions mentioned see pages 4–5.

Taxation was the single most important cause of unrest in the early Tudor period. People objected to increased or **innovative taxation** demands, either because new demands indicated unwelcome increased control from central government, or because people simply could not afford to pay.

It was the main cause of unrest in the revolts of 1489, 1497 and 1525 and a minor cause in 1536 and 1549. After 1549 it was not an issue, although the heavy tax demands caused by the Spanish war may have played a role in the Oxfordshire Rising of 1596 (see page 18).

Henry VII (1485–1509)

Henry's weak position and dynastic threats meant he needed to raise money to secure his position. In 1489 Parliament voted for £100,000 in taxation to fund a war in France and in 1497 they voted for an additional £60,000 to fund a war against the Scots. This led to regional rebellions from Yorkshire and Cornwall, as they objected to paying taxes to fund wars which did not concern them, indicating that **provincialism** was strong in England.

Loyalty to local area

Yorkshire Rebellion (1489)

Protestors in Yorkshire objected to paying for a war in France that did not concern them and to paying a tax from which they were traditionally exempt because they had to pay for defence of the northern borders against the Scots. The north was also very poor and the situation was made worse by a bad harvest in 1488. Henry refused to negotiate despite other northern counties being excluded from the tax due to their poverty, and the rebels murdered the tax collector, the Earl of Northumberland. An army was sent, which easily defeated the rebels.

Cornish Rebellion (1497)

As in Yorkshire, the Cornish objected to paying for wars that did not concern them, this time against the Scots and Perkin Warbeck (see page 6). The rebels claimed their grievances were against royal officials who advised the King on finance, John Morton and Reginald Bray. The threat was serious as the rebels raised 15,000 men and marched to Blackheath in London. A royal army was sent and the rebels were defeated.

Henry VIII (1509–47)

The Amicable Grant Rising (1525)

Without permi... of Parliame...

The Amicable Grant was a **non-parliamentary tax** which followed a period of heavy taxation as England was at war with France. As a result of **forced loans** in 1522 and a **subsidy** in 1523 many people were financially exhausted and there had been little territorial gain in Henry's earlier wars in the 1510s. The grant was based on assessments made by government officials and ended the concept of a **fixed rate** so that many were paying taxes at a higher rate than previously. It also came at a time of worsening economic conditions. There were protests in many counties, but larger risings in Suffolk. The difficulty in collecting the money forced the government to back down and the ringleaders were pardoned.

The Pilgrimage of Grace (1536–37)

Only one of the rebels' **Articles** in the Pilgrimage of Grace (see page 4) concerned taxation. They demanded that the **Subsidy Act** of 1534 was abandoned. The rebels argued that the tax was innovative as it was not being raised for the defence of the realm.

Edward VI: The Western Rebellion (1549)

The Western Rebellion in 1549 (see pages 4–5) opposed the Subsidy Act of 1549 which aimed to raise money on sheep and woollen cloth. This would have hit farmers in the West Country, where sheep farming predominated, particularly hard. The tax was due to be assessed just after the introduction of the new **Prayer Book**, which was also resented.

Spot the mistake

Below are a sample exam question and a paragraph written in answer to this question. Why does this paragraph not get into at least Level IB? Once you have identified the mistake, rewrite the paragraph so that it displays the qualities of at least Level IB. The mark scheme on page 3 will help you.

> 'Taxation was the most important cause of social and economic unrest in the period from 1485 to 1603.' How far do you agree?

Taxation caused the Yorkshire Rebellion in 1489. The rebels objected to paying taxes to fund Henry VII's war in France. The northern counties were usually exempt from such taxes as they were expected to pay for the defence of the northern borders against Scottish attacks. They also felt that the war against France did not concern them and therefore the tax was unfair. Yorkshire also objected as other northern counties had been exempted from the tax because of poverty.

Spider diagram

Use the information on the opposite page and your own knowledge to add detail to the spider diagram below.

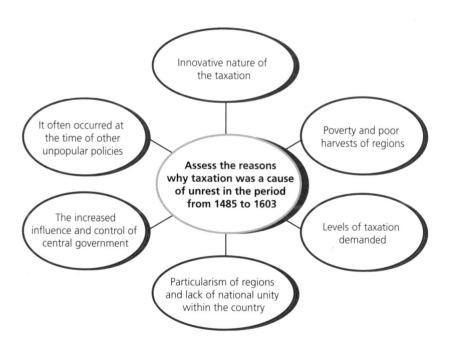

Religion

Chang of of religion [handwritten margin note]

For a description of all the rebellions mentioned see pages 4–5.

Religion became a cause of rebellion as a result of the **Reformation**. Until the 1530s religion had been a unifying factor, helping to increase political stability, but it was a major cause of two rebellions and played a role of varying importance in four other rebellions in the period between 1536 and 1569. Most rebellions with religion as a cause wanted to reverse the religious changes, with Kett's being the exception. However, by the end of the period it was no longer a cause of unrest as most people accepted the Elizabethan Church.

Henry VIII: The Pilgrimage of Grace (1536–37)

The Pilgrimage comprised three separate risings in northern England. They were in response to **visitations** by Church commissioners to investigate the clergy and close smaller monasteries. This also caused rumours of attacks on parish churches. The rebels argued that the closure of the monasteries affected not only religious provision, but the social and economic services provided by them. In addition, monasteries often acted as a church for local people and their closure would have had an impact on local church attendance. The rebel demands reflected this concern. Nine of the twenty-four demands were about religious grievances, including the attack on saints, holy days and pilgrimages as well as monasteries. The rising had many religious symbols with the rebels carrying a banner of the **Five Wounds of Christ** and singing the **Pilgrims' ballad**.

Edward VI (1547–53)

The Western Rebellion (1549)

As well as its economic causes (see page 10) the Western Rebellion seemed to be a reaction to the changes brought about by the Edwardian reformation, particularly the introduction of the 1549 Prayer Book. Thirteen demands were religious and called for a restoration of traditional Catholic practices: the Latin mass, **relics**, images and **chantries**. However, they did not call for the restoration of the **papacy**. — *authent of the office of the pope* [handwritten margin note]

Kett's Rebellion (1549)

Although this was largely a social protest (see page 16), the rebels did complain about the lack of progress of the Reformation and called for an improvement in the quality of the clergy.

Mary Tudor (1553–58)

Lady Jane Grey (1553)

Although the move to put Lady Jane Grey on the throne was largely political (see page 5), it could be argued that the leaders of the movement were concerned that Mary's accession would lead to a Catholic restoration and therefore rose to defend the changes brought about under Edward.

Wyatt's Rebellion (1554)

Thomas Wyatt claimed the rising was not religious, but this may have been an attempt to widen support to include Catholics opposed to Mary's marriage. However, it took place in a strongly Protestant area and people knew that Mary was strongly attached to Catholicism. There were fears her marriage would result in the re-establishment of a Catholic dynasty.

Elizabeth I: The Northern Earls (1569)

The Earl of Northumberland claimed the first aim of the rebellion was to reform religion. Indeed, the two leaders, Northumberland and Westmorland, were both Catholic. However, it may well have been a cloak for political motives. Nevertheless, there were many religious elements to the rebellion, with the rebels using the banner of the Five Wounds, restoring mass in Durham Cathedral, destroying **English Bibles** and setting up **stone altars**.

Develop the detail

Below is a sample exam question and paragraph written in answer to this question. The paragraph contains a limited amount of detail. Annotate the paragraph to add additional detail to the answer.

'Religion was the most common cause of rebellion in England throughout the period 1485–1603.' How far do you agree with this view?

Religion was a cause of rebellion only during the middle part of the period. It was only when Henry VIII introduced religious changes that it became a cause of unrest as before then the country was religiously united. Religion was a particularly important cause of the Pilgrimage of Grace under Henry VIII, although there were other causes of this rebellion as well. It continued to be an important cause of rebellion under Edward VI, most notably in the Western Rebellion, where the rebels wanted to reverse the changes he had introduced. However, it was also a minor cause of Kett's Rebellion, where the rebels complained about the clergy. The last rebellion where religion was important was the rebellion of the Northern Earls, who had similar religious symbols to the Pilgrims and restored traditional practices. However, after this rebellion religion played no further role in causing unrest, unlike other factors which remained a cause throughout the period.

Introducing an argument

Below are a sample exam question, a list of key points to be made in the essay, and a simple introduction and conclusion for the essay. Read these and then, using the information on the opposite page, earlier in the section and on page 14, rewrite the introduction and the conclusion in order to develop an argument.

Assess the reasons why religion was a cause of unrest only in the period from 1536 to 1569.

Key points:

- Lack of noticeable religious change before 1536
- Preserve traditional practices
- Link to succession and faction
- Elizabethan Religious Settlement
- Cloak for political motives

Introduction

There were many reasons why religion was a cause of unrest only in the period from 1536 to 1569. These reasons were linked to politics, faction and the succession as well as religious issues. It is also important to consider why there was no religious unrest in the periods before 1536 and after 1569. This was because of the lack of religious change. All of these factors help to explain why religion was a cause of unrest only between 1536 and 1569.

Conclusion

To conclude, there were many reasons why religion was a cause of unrest only in the period from 1536 to 1569. These reasons were linked to politics, faction and the succession as well as religious issues. The context in which the religious changes were made was also important. However, the most important reason was the nature of the religious changes in the period from 1536 to 1569.

Faction

> For a description of all the rebellions mentioned see pages 4–5.

The emergence of a small group of councillors from whom the monarch took advice led to the formation of **factions**. Councillors whose advice was ignored or who were not rewarded with patronage formed opposition groups and tried to replace those in positions of influence. This was possibly the most common cause of unrest throughout the period and can be seen as a cause of most rebellions, although often a secondary, rather than a primary cause. These factions turned to rebellion when all other attempts to achieve influence had failed.

Henry VII (1485–1509)

Although associated with dynastic unrest (see page 6), the Yorkists (the Lovel, Stafford and Pretender Rebellions) acted like a faction. They wanted to remove both the monarch and the 'evil councillors', such as Bray and Morton (see page 10), who advised him.

Henry VIII (1509–47)

The Amicable Grant Rising (1525)

It has been suggested that a major cause of the failure to raise the Amicable Grant was factional as those opposed to Cardinal Wolsey, who dominated the court, used the original opposition to the tax to stir up further unrest and made little effort to collect the tax. This allowed opposition to spread and opponents of Wolsey hoped that Henry would lose faith in his minister.

The Pilgrimage of Grace (1536–37)

It has been argued that the motivation behind the Pilgrimage of Grace was factional. The **Aragonese** faction, supporters of Catherine of Aragon and her daughter, Mary Tudor, wanted to regain influence. The rebellion attempted to remove Henry's chief minister, Thomas **Cromwell**. Many of the leaders, such as Lord Thomas Darcy and Lord John Hussey had links with Catherine. They hoped to restore Mary to the succession.

Mary Tudor (1553–58)

Lady Jane Grey (1553)

It could be argued that the attempt to alter the succession in favour of Lady Jane Grey (see page 5) was an attempt to preserve the domination of Northumberland's supporters, knowing they would lose influence when Mary came to the throne.

Wyatt's Rebellion (1554)

Originally, the rebellion was supposed to be a four-pronged attack on the capital, led by many who would have lost, or feared they would lose, influence at court with the marriage of Mary to Philip of Spain. Men, such as Wyatt, who had served earlier monarchs feared they would lose their positions and influence to Spaniards who would be rewarded following the marriage.

Elizabeth I (1558–1603)

The Northern Earls (1569)

Northumberland and Westmorland were losing influence both at court and in the North as southern councillors, led by William Cecil, dominated court and were brought into government in the North. They blamed him for the religious changes and the foreign policy that appeared to be taking England closer to war, as well as for the uncertainty over the succession. This led to their plan to marry Mary Queen of Scots to the Duke of Norfolk and force Elizabeth to recognise her as heir.

The Earl of Essex (1601)

A former favourite of Elizabeth, the Earl of Essex had been suspended from the **Privy Council** and banned from Court, where Robert Cecil dominated. His position was in decline and he was unable to provide rewards for his supporters such as the Earl of Southampton. He believed that a demonstration in London would have support and force Elizabeth to restore his influence.

Spectrum of significance

Below is a sample exam question and a list of general points which could be used to answer part of the question. Use your own knowledge and the information on the opposite page and from the rest of this section to reach a judgement about the importance of these general points to the question posed. Write the numbers on the spectrum below to indicate their relative importance. Having done this, write a brief justification of your placement, explaining why some of these factors are more important than others. The resulting diagram could form the basis of an essay plan.

'Faction was the most important cause of unrest throughout the period from 1485 to 1603.' How far do you agree with this view?

1   Faction

2   Heavy taxation

3   Religious changes

4   Dynastic challenges to the throne

5   Economic and social problems

6   Increased government centralisation

Most important   Least important

Developing an argument

Below is a sample exam question, a list of key points to be made in the essay, and a paragraph from the essay. Read the question, the key points and the sample paragraph. Using the information from the opposite page and from earlier in this section rewrite the paragraph in order to develop an argument. Your paragraph should explain why the factor discussed in the paragraph is either the most significant factor or less significant than another factor.

'Faction was the most serious cause of unrest throughout the period 1485–1603.' How far do you agree?

Key points:

● Factional disputes threatened every Tudor monarch **but** …

● Factional disputes attracted limited support.

● Dynastic unrest forced the monarch into battle.

● Taxation rebellions often attracted large numbers and forced a change in policy.

Sample paragraph

Factional unrest affected every Tudor monarch. Henry VII faced challenges from the Yorkist faction following his victory at Bosworth. Simnel and his 3000 mercenaries fought Henry at Stoke and there was further factional conflict with Warbeck and Lovel and Stafford. There were also taxation rebellions in Yorkshire and Cornwall. These rebellions forced the government to abandon the taxes. Under Henry VIII the large-scale rising against the Amicable Grant was to prevent further taxes, but it also attacked the king's chief minister, Wolsey. The 40,000 who rose in the Pilgrimage of Grace were mostly concerned by religious changes but also attacked Cromwell and attempted to restore the influence of Catherine of Aragon's supporters. Wyatt's Rebellion, which attracted 5000, was a response to the Spanish marriage and fears that courtiers would lose their positions. During Elizabeth's reign the Northern Earls rose with 5000 men, but fled when royal forces approached. Essex raised a few hundred men in his protest against his loss of influence. The city of London did not rise to support him.

Famine, inflation and social issues

For a description of all the rebellions mentioned see pages 4–5.

Many of the riots throughout the period were the result of social and economic tensions. They were often the triggers for localised unrest, and if not put down quickly, could become major rebellions.

Famine and disease

Although one in four harvests failed and resulted in increased mortality and price rises, there is only one obvious example of this resulting in open rebellion – the Oxfordshire Rising of 1596 (see pages 18–19). However, there were examples of **food riots**, particularly during Elizabeth's reign in the 1580s and 1590s, with riots in Gloucestershire and Hampshire in 1586 and Somerset, Sussex and Kent in 1596–97.

Similarly, despite at least four outbreaks of plague and **the sweat** there was no associated unrest.

It appears that in times of famine and disease potential rebels stayed at home to look after their crops, whilst the **yeomen** and **gentry**, who might have led unrest, benefited from the subsequent rise in the price of food.

Inflation and rents

workers relying on wage into income

Inflation was an increasing problem from the 1520s onwards and had a serious impact on the price of grain, which rose faster than wages. This was largely the result of a rising population which increased demand for grain. **Wage labourers** suffered the most and inflation did play a role in some rebellions in the mid century. Landowners raised rents to try and make up for the losses caused by inflation and often evicted those who could not pay.

The Pilgrimage of Grace (1536–37)

The Pilgrims wanted **entry fines** to be set at two years' rent. This would prevent landlords making up for their losses from rents, caused by inflation, by charging more to new **tenants**. The rebels also argued that the closure of the monasteries would hit the poor who relied on monastic charity.

Kett's Rebellion (1549)

The rebels had the unrealistic demand that the price of land and rent for land be returned to that of 1485. Similar to the Pilgrims, they also wanted entry fines to be controlled. Some landlords had also revived old feudal dues, such as **castleward**, which the rebels protested against.

Social issues

Social issues were a major cause of the unrest that gripped England in 1549, resulting in what has been described as 'commotion time' or 'camping time' as the rebels often established camps from which they attempted to control the local area. There was unrest in 26 counties in central and southern England. Social grievances were clearly present in the demands of both Kett's Rebellion and the Western rebels. It does appear that in both rebellions the rebels wanted to narrow the gap between the rich and the peasants.

Kett's Rebellion (1549)

Seventeen of the twenty-nine demands were linked to rents, landlords and **enclosures** (see pages 18–19). The rebels' targets were landlords and this rebellion was the closest thing to 'class war' seen in this period, as most land was owned by a small number of nobles and gentry. The rebels wanted **serfs** to be set free and a number of the demands specifically attacked offices of local government, which were held by gentry. There were criticisms of rabbit warrens and dovecotes, again symbols of gentry status.

The Western Rebellion (1549)

Although there were no demands regarding rents, the rebels attacked gentry at St Michael's Mount and Trematon suggesting that class war was not far below the surface. The demands included a call to limit the size of gentry households.

Support or challenge?

Below is a sample exam question which asks how far you agree with a specific statement. Below this are a series of general statements which are relevant to the question. Using your own knowledge of the whole period and the information on the opposite page decide whether these statements support or challenge the statement in the question and tick the appropriate box.

'Social problems were a greater cause of unrest in the period up to 1549 than in the period from 1549 to 1603.' How far do you agree with this view?

	SUPPORT	CHALLENGE
There was little unrest caused by social issues during the reign of Henry VII.		
The Pilgrims demanded that entry fines were set at two years' rent.		
Outbreaks of plague and the sweat never directly caused unrest.		
Kett's rebels wanted the price of land and rents to be returned to 1485 levels.		
Unrest in 1549 affected 26 counties in southern and central England.		
The Western rebels attacked local gentry.		
Food riots broke out in many areas of southern England in the 1580s and 1590s.		
The only evidence of poor harvests causing unrest is the Oxfordshire Rising of 1596.		

Introducing an argument

Below are a sample exam question, a list of key points to be made in the essay, and a simple introduction and conclusion for the essay. Read these and then, using the information on the opposite page and from earlier in the section, rewrite the introduction and the conclusion in order to develop an argument.

'Rarely the trigger, but frequently the underlying cause.' How far do you agree with this view of the role of social and economic grievances as a cause of unrest in the period from 1485 to 1603?

Key points:

- What is meant by 'trigger' and 'underlying cause'
- Social grievances – class discontent
- Economic grievances – poor harvests, inflation, enclosure
- Trigger causes of unrest – enclosure, religious change, dynastic
- Underlying causes – inflation, religious change, poverty, faction

Introduction

I partly agree that social and economic causes were rarely the trigger, but they were frequently the underlying cause of unrest. In some rebellions social and economic causes acted as the trigger, but in other rebellions other factors were more important. Social and economic grievances were often the underlying cause, but in some rebellions this was not the case.

Conclusion

Social and economic grievances were rarely the trigger for unrest but often the underlying cause to an extent. They were not the trigger when class discontent caused unrest, but were when enclosure was a cause. They were important as underlying causes because of inflation and poor harvests, but religious changes and loss of influence were also important.

Enclosure

> For a description of all the rebellions mentioned see pages 4–5.

Although enclosure was not often a major cause of unrest, it did cause tensions between landowners and tenants, particularly when land was converted from **arable** to **pasture**, resulting in less demand for labour, or when **common land** was fenced off. When this was done amicably there was little trouble. However, despite this, enclosure did play a role in the events of 1536, 1549 and 1596, and had caused some local unrest in 1510.

Henry VIII: The Pilgrimage of Grace (1536–37)

One of the rebel demands called for the pulling down of enclosures put up since 1489, except in regions of mountains, forests and parks. There had been enclosure riots in 1535 and it was likely this was a grievance in certain areas of the North, particularly in lowlands where the population had been rising and there was increased pressure on land.

Edward VI: The 'commotion time' (1549)

Enclosure played a role in most of the 26 counties where unrest took place in 1549. It was a particular problem in the **sheep-corn areas** of the Midlands, East Anglia and the South and South East, where population pressure and land shortage added to the tensions. Encouraged by the **Duke of Somerset's Enclosure Commission**, many tenants took the law into their own hands and pulled down fences and hedges. The first rising, at Northaw in Hertfordshire, in May 1548, was over enclosure and may have been the prelude to the other risings. This can be seen in the following examples:

- Wiltshire – Lord Herbert's hedges pulled down at Wilton.
- Sussex – Earl of Arundel forced some gentlemen to take down hedges to stop riots.
- Surrey – Hedges at Witley Park pulled down.

Kett's Rebellion (1549)

The first article of Kett's demands attacked enclosure and the rebellion was triggered by a dispute between landowners Robert Kett and John Flowerdew who had recently enclosed land. Kett took down his own fences before the rebels did and led the attack on Flowerdew's lands. Landlords appeared to be obstructing an enquiry into illegal enclosure and the rebels may have believed that they would have government support in attacking enclosures. However, the demands were not simply anti-enclosure: the first demand protected enclosures where saffron was grown and many tenants supported enclosure when it prevented landowners from **folding cattle** on their land. The biggest concern was when wealthy landowners took over common land or pastured large flocks on it as it denied peasants the right to use the land.

The Western Rebellion (1549)

Although enclosure was not mentioned in the demands of this rebellion, contemporaries did comment on the problem of enclosure and mentioned the pulling down of hedges.

Elizabeth I: The Oxfordshire Rising (1596)

The government had lifted the restrictions on enclosing open fields in 1593 as there was plenty of cheap grain available. As a result, there were new enclosures in Oxfordshire at Hampton Gaye and Hampton Poyle. This was one of the reasons why an assembly was arranged in 1596 at Enslow Hill, the site of the 1549 rising sparked by enclosures. This time, however, it failed to attract numbers and only four men turned up.

In 1607 the widespread Midland enclosure revolt took place, indicating that enclosure was still an issue.

Identify an argument a

Below are a series of definitions, a sample exam question and two sample conclusions. One of the conclusions achieves a high level because it contains an argument. The other achieves a lower level because it contains only description and assertion. Identify which is which. The mark scheme on page 3 will help you.

- **Description:** a detailed account
- **Assertion:** a statement of fact or an opinion which is not supported by a reason
- **Reason:** a statement that explains or justifies something
- **Argument:** an assertion justified with a reason

How important was enclosure as a cause of unrest in the period from 1485 to 1603?

Sample 1

Enclosure was not a major cause of rebellion, but it did cause tensions, particularly when landowners encroached on common land or converted land from arable to pasture. Enclosure caused local riots, as in the 1510s, 1540s and 1590s, however only a few became serious, particularly in 1549. Enclosure was a major cause of Kett's Rebellion in 1549, when the rebels threw down the hedges of John Flowerdew, and some of the other minor disturbances, as at Witley. However, in 1536 complaint against enclosure was only one of the grievances of the Pilgrims, whereas in 1596 only four people rose in Oxfordshire over enclosure grievances. Enclosure may have been an underlying grievance, but it was rarely the major cause of unrest.

Sample 2

There had been much rioting in the North over enclosure in 1535. Enclosure then appeared as a grievance in the list of demands drawn up by the Pilgrims in 1536. Kett's Rebellion followed rivalry between two landowners, Robert Kett and John Flowerdew. Both had enclosed lands, but Kett pulled down his fences; he then led men to attack Flowerdew's fences. There were also further examples of hedges being pulled down in Surrey and the Home Counties. In 1593 the government lifted the restrictions on enclosing open fields, but in 1596 following enclosure in Oxfordshire, four men gathered at Enslow Hill. These events show that enclosure was a frequent cause of unrest throughout the period.

 Turning assertion into argument a

Below is a sample exam question and a series of assertions. Read the question and then add a justification to each of the assertions to turn each one into an argument.

Assess the importance of enclosure as a cause of social and economic unrest in the period from 1485 to 1603.

Enclosure was a significant cause of social and economic unrest because it led to

_____

However, in many social and economic rebellions enclosure was often just the trigger because

_____

Also, enclosure unrest often failed to raise large numbers because

_____

Ireland

> For a description of all the rebellions mentioned see pages 4–5.

The revolts in Ireland were largely the result of attempts by the government in England to increase central control. In that sense they were similar to the tax revolts of 1489, 1497 and 1525 (see page 10), and the rebellions of the Pilgrims in 1536 and the Northern Earls in 1569. Like the Irish, these groups felt that their traditional rights and privileges were being ignored.

Until 1534 the monarch had worked with the Earl of Kildare, who was **Deputy Lieutenant**, and there were no rebellions. However, the period 1534–1603 saw five major rebellions (see below), all primarily caused by increased government intervention.

Henry VIII (1509–47)

From 1532 onwards Thomas Cromwell, the king's chief minister, began to change the distribution of power in Ireland and Kildare started to lose influence. The crucial issues were the religious changes that followed Henry VIII being made Head of the Church. The King doubted Kildare would uphold his new title. Kildare was summoned to England, but lodged in the Tower of London where he died, which prompted his son and uncles to rise in rebellion.

The Silken Thomas Rebellion (1534–37)

Kildare's son, Thomas O'Neill (also known as **Silken Thomas**), ignored similar requests to come to London to discuss policy and instead raised 1000 men and invaded the **Pale**. Although the rebels attacked the religious changes, the primary cause of the unrest was political as Silken wanted to drive the English out and become ruler in Ireland.

Elizabeth I (1558–1603)

It was during the reign of Elizabeth that the majority of Irish rebellions occurred as the government attempted to increase its influence in Ireland and reduce the power of the clan chiefs.

Although all the rebellions were politically motivated against increased English control, religion and the defence of the Catholic Church were often used to gain wider support.

Shane O'Neill (1558–67)

O'Neill wanted to rule **Ulster** and killed his own brother to achieve this. Elizabeth forgave him, but he was soon plotting with France and Mary Queen of Scots. Although he claimed to be acting as defender of the Catholic faith, his aim was to increase his power.

Fitzgerald Rebellion (1569–73)

James Fitzmaurice Fitzgerald resented English attempts to colonise Ireland (and the settlers' brutal treatment of the Irish) and the imposition of martial law, both of which increased English influence. He was particularly annoyed that his cousin had been put in the Tower of London following a feud with the English Butler clan. Although he also claimed to be defending Catholicism from Elizabeth's religious changes, it was the growing English influence that was the main cause.

Geraldine Rebellion (1579–83)

The main cause of unrest was the hatred towards the increasing number of English settlers and increased government interference from Dublin into clan life. However, in order to increase support Fitzgerald also appealed to the growing animosity to the religious changes that had followed Elizabeth's **excommunication** and the 1569–73 rebellion.

Tyrone (1595–1603)

The **plantation system** caused increased hostility between the Irish and the English as the settlers raised rents, took over more land and began to establish the Protestant Church. In 1595 Tyrone led a revolt, which soon became nationwide, with the aim of removing the settlers and the English administration so that Ireland could become independent. Tyrone also had his own personal grievance as he felt he had not been properly rewarded by the English government for helping them when the government in Ireland was attacked by other clans.

Simple essay style

Below is a sample exam question. Use your own knowledge, information on the opposite page and information from other sections of the book to produce a plan for this question. Choose four general points, and provide three pieces of specific information to support each general point. Once you have planned your essay, write the introduction and conclusion for the essay. The introduction should list the points to be discussed in the essay and outline the line of argument you intend to take. The conclusion should summarise the key points and justify which point was the most important.

To what extent were the causes of Irish rebellion similar to those in England in the period from 1485 to 1603?

Recommended reading

Irish rebellions are often neglected by students. However, it is worth spending time studying them in some depth as it enhances understanding of patterns of change and continuity. Below is a list of suggested further reading on this topic.

- *Access to History: Rebellion and Disorder under the Tudors 1485–1603*, pages viii–x, 6–8, Geoff Woodward (2008)

- *Advanced History Core Texts: The Reign of Elizabeth, England 1558–1603*, pages 93–100, Barbara Mervyn (2001)

- *Access to History: Elizabeth I: Religion and Foreign Affairs*, Chapter 6, John Warren (2002)

Why did rebellions occur?

For a description of all the rebellions mentioned see pages 4–5.

In the previous pages we have tried to group the rebellions, but it should be clear that very few rebellions had just one cause, although some patterns do emerge. The table below outlines the pattern of unrest, showing when particular causes dominated.

THEME	OCCURRENCE	EXAMPLE
Dynastic	Predominantly a cause in the early period, when Tudor claim was weak and Yorkists challenged it. Less important from 1530s	Lovel, Warbeck, Simnel
Taxation	Major cause under Henry VII and early Henry VIII, subsidiary after 1525	Yorkshire, Cornwall, Amicable Grant
Religion	Only a cause once Reformation started and no religious unrest after 1569	Pilgrimage of Grace, Western
Faction	A cause throughout the period from Yorkists under Henry VII to the rebellion against the Cecil faction under Elizabeth	Yorkist unrest under Henry VII, Pilgrimage of Grace, Northern Earls, Essex
Economic and social	Often an underlying cause, but most significant in 1549	Kett
Enclosure	Underlying cause in 1536, but most significant in 1549 and 1596	Kett, Oxfordshire
Ireland	Mostly occur under Elizabeth as a reaction to increased government interference	Fitzgerald, Tyrone

Monocausal

Very few rebellions had just one cause. The taxation unrest under Henry VII and Henry VIII and the dynastic unrest under Henry VII may be seen as such, as could the Irish rebellions, with their resentment at English rule. However, even in some of these there were other underlying causes, with religion in Ireland and faction in some of the taxation unrest.

Multicausal

Some themes, such as faction, are present throughout the period, but their relative importance varies. In the religious rebellions, such as the Pilgrimage of Grace, there is evidence of factional conflict, social and economic grievance and even dynastic concerns and a similar pattern can be seen in the rebellion of the Northern Earls.

The 1549 commotions in the West Country and in East Anglia appear very different, with the West Country risings having mainly religious causes whereas those in East Anglia had social and economic causes. However, the West Country also had social and economic grievances with the sheep tax, whilst Kett had complaints about the quality of the clergy.

Motives

It is important to distinguish between the causes of unrest and the motives of the rebels. Sometimes, the demands may not reflect the true motives of the rebels and these may be best revealed by looking at their actions.

Long-term/Short-term causes

The rebellions often had long-term grievances, but needed a trigger to spark the unrest. In the Pilgrimage of Grace and the Western Rebellion the underlying causes were the disruption caused by religious change and social and economic pressures. The trigger in the Pilgrimage of Grace may have been the rumour of changes to the parish church and the closure of small monasteries, and in the Western Rebellion it might have been the introduction of the Prayer Book.

In many of the rebellions the underlying cause appears to be social and economic. The period saw rising prices and population causing increased pressures on the peasantry. However, another event was usually needed to spark unrest.

REBELLION	MAIN CAUSE AS SHOWN IN THE DEMANDS	MOTIVES AS REVEALED BY ACTIONS
Pilgrimage of Grace	Religion, demand for restoration of the monasteries and traditional practices, such as holy days	Religion as rebels re-open monasteries. So, in this case, the demands and motives are the same.
Kett	Changes to economic and social policy of the government	Anti-gentry as they attack the gentry and hold some as prisoners
Western	Changes to religious policy, particularly the new Prayer Book	Anti-gentry as they shout 'Kill the gentlemen' and murder a member of the local gentry

Complete the paragraph

Below are a sample exam question and a paragraph written in answer to this question. The paragraph contains a point and specific examples, but lacks a concluding explanatory link back to the question. Using the information from the opposite page and the whole section complete the paragraph adding this link in the space provided.

'Most rebellions in the period from 1485 to 1603 had more than one cause.' How far do you agree?

> Rebellions in the period seldom had just one cause. This is seen most clearly in rebellions such as the Pilgrimage of Grace and Western Rebellion. Both rebellions had religion as their main cause, with the Pilgrims demanding the restoration of smaller monasteries and the Western demanding the abolition of the new Prayer Book. Both rebellions also wanted to protect traditional practices, such as holy days and the use of holy bread and water. The rebellions also had religious symbols as both marched under the banner of the Five Wounds of Christ. However, the rebels also had social and economic grievances about taxation, with the Pilgrims complaining about the Subsidy Act and the Western rebels about the Sheep Tax.
>
> _____
>
> _____
>
> _____

 Simple essay style

Below is a sample exam question. Use your own knowledge, information on the opposite page and information from other sections of the book to produce a plan for this question. Choose four general points, and provide three pieces of specific information to support each general point. Once you have planned your essay, write the introduction and conclusion for the essay. The introduction should list the points to be discussed in the essay and outline the line of argument you intend to take. The conclusion should summarise the key points and justify which point was the most important.

To what extent did the causes of rebellion remain the same throughout the period 1485–1603?

Section 2: The frequency and nature of disturbances

> For a description of all the rebellions mentioned see pages 4–5.

Most rebellions took place in **peripheral** regions of the kingdom, in part because these places were furthest away from central government in London and the king was more dependent upon local nobles and gentry to maintain order there.

The North

At the start of the period the North was a Yorkist stronghold as it had been Richard III's seat of power. Lovel and Stafford attempted to raise forces there in 1486. The 1489 tax rebellion had some Yorkist links, but was also the result of the region's **particularism** in not paying taxes, except to defend the Scottish border. The Pilgrimage of Grace in 1536–37 and the rebellion of the Northern Earls in 1569 were in part a response to resentment at the growing power of London and the region's exclusion from decision-making. The northern nobles felt their status had been undermined.

The South West

The South West was not concerned about dynastic issues, but resented the increased role of central government, particularly with regards to taxation. Cultural and linguistic differences, particularly in Cornwall, may have given the region a sense of difference and encouraged resistance to taxation and religious innovation.

East Anglia

There was a tradition of unrest in East Anglia, with outbreaks in 1381 during the **Peasants' Revolt**, **enclosure** riots in 1525 and attacks on the gentry in 1540, before the major uprising in 1549. The rebels established a series of camps in places where local government was administered, such as Bury St Edmunds.

Ireland

The distance from London and the difficulty of sending troops encouraged unrest. This grew as the period progressed because the government increased its control over the region – challenging the traditional clan power of families such as Tyrone, O'Neill and Fitzgerald. The attempt under Elizabeth to introduce Protestantism and the **plantation system** caused further problems.

Major towns and cities

In many of the disturbances the rebels attempted to seize the capital or the regional or religious centre. The Cornish (1497) and Wyatt (1554) rebellions both marched to London, whilst Essex attempted his rising there in 1601. The Pilgrims seized York, the regional capital of the North in October 1536, whilst Lincoln, the seat of the local bishop, was taken earlier, in October 1536. Similarly, the Northern Earls entered the religious centre of Durham to restore mass in 1569. In 1549, Kett's rebels seized Norwich, the regional capital of East Anglia, and the Western rebels besieged Exeter, the regional capital of the South West, although they failed to take it.

Tradition

Some rebels focused on sites of earlier unrest. The Cornish went to Blackheath in June 1497, where the Peasants' Revolt had gathered in 1381. The Western Rebellion (1549) started at Bodmin, as had the Cornish Rebellion of 1497. The Oxfordshire Rising of 1596 gathered at Enslow Hill, which had been the site of a gathering in 1549.

The importance of the nobility

Areas were more likely to witness unrest if the relationship between the nobility and inhabitants was poor. This was seen in 1549 in the West Country where Lord John Russell had newly replaced the Courtenays, and in East Anglia where the Howards had fallen from power. Where control was strong, unrest was limited, for example in Sussex where the Earl of Arundel ruled.

Develop the detail

Below are a sample exam question and a paragraph written in answer to this question. The paragraph contains a limited amount of detail. Annotate the paragraph to add additional detail to the answer.

'Rebellions always attempted to seize regional capitals.' Assess this view.

> Many rebellions throughout the period attempted to seize regional capitals. Regional capitals were administrative centres and their seizure presented a direct challenge to the government which would have to send in troops to regain control as happened in 1549. Regional capitals were often the seats of the local bishops and in religious protests the rebels wanted to control these. However, they were not always successful in taking them, even when they laid siege to them. It was not just regional capitals that the rebels attempted to seize. Many rebellions attempted to take the capital city itself because it was the centre of government. The situation in Ireland was very different as the rebel tactics were not the same and the seizure of major towns or cities did not occur.

Introducing an argument

Below are a sample exam question, a list of key points to be made in the essay, and a simple introduction and conclusion for the essay. Read these and then, using the information from the page opposite and from the rest of this section, rewrite the introduction and the conclusion in order to develop an argument.

'Rebellion was more frequent in regions furthest from London.' How far do you agree with this view?

Key points:
- The regions which are furthest from London: Ireland, the North and West
- Unrest in London and East Anglia
- Nature of rebellion and distance from London
- Pattern of change over time?
- Policies in the peripheral regions

Introduction

> To an extent rebellion was more frequent in the regions furthest away from London. The regions furthest from London were accustomed to greater freedom and often saw themselves as almost independent, particularly during the early period when particularism and regionalism were very strong. However, unrest in London and East Anglia was also quite common.

Conclusion

> Rebellion was to some extent more frequent in the peripheral areas. Despite government policies, rebellion remained a constant threat. However, there were other areas, such as London, that saw unrest in the final years of Elizabeth's reign.

The size, frequency and duration

For a description of all the rebellions mentioned see pages 4–5.

Size of rebellions

The size of rebellions varied greatly, ranging from just four people in the Oxfordshire Rising (1596) to around 40,000 in the Pilgrimage of Grace (1536–37). After the crisis of 1549, when perhaps 15,000 rebels entered Norwich under Kett, the numbers declined (see table).

Date	Rebellion	Numbers
1497	Cornwall	15,000
1525	Amicable Grant	10,000
1536–37	Pilgrimage of Grace	40,000
1549	Kett	15,000
1554	Wyatt	5,000
1569	Northern Earls	5,000
1601	Essex	300

This decline was perhaps a result of the failure of rebellions or because the social groups that often led rebellions were incorporated into the state through offices such as **Poor Law** administrators. This meant that later rebellions were usually led by nobles who were either impoverished or excluded and felt they had nothing to lose. These rebellions were also more often about **high politics** that did not rouse popular support.

Numbers involved in Irish rebellions were usually small, but Tyrone's Rebellion was the exception as he was able to raise 6000.

Frequency

There were two periods when rebellion was most frequent.

1 Under Henry VII, because he was insecure and had gained the throne by force. There were alternative claimants and foreign powers were willing to support them. Henry needed money to defeat the threats and raised taxes causing further unrest.

2 The mid-Tudor period (1536–54) because the Crown was weak due to religious turmoil and rule by a minor and a female. This coincided with a period of rising prices and social problems.

Under Elizabeth (1558–1603) the frequency of rebellions in England declined because:

- The Tudors became more secure and removed rival claimants, such as the Poles, the leading Yorkist family with a claim to the throne. The Countess of Salisbury was executed in 1541 by Henry VIII.

- The **Elizabethan Religious Settlement** were moderate and helped to remove religious tensions that had caused unrest in the mid-Tudor period.

- Social and economic problems peaked in the 1540s and, although the 1590s were a time of economic hardship, government legislation, such as the Poor Law, helped to lessen the impact.

- The role of **JPs** and **Lord Lieutenants** were developed under Mary and Elizabeth; they helped to deal with issues at a local level.

- The gentry became less willing to lead rebellions and were incorporated into serving the state as JPs.

- Parliament and law courts were used more frequently to resolve disputes.

Duration

Although there appears to be no overall pattern to the duration of rebellions, a few points do emerge:

- Rebellions further away from London lasted longer because of the time taken to raise and send a force:
  - Irish unrest often lasted years.
  - Rebellions in the North and South West lasted longer than those in other regions, for example the Cornish Rebellion over a month, the Pilgrimage of Grace and the Western Rebellion over two months.

- Government underestimation of the seriousness of rebellions resulted in their taking longer to suppress. This was the case in Kett's Rebellion of 1549.

- Rebellions near or in London lasted a short time as they threatened the seat of government. Consequently, the government raised troops quickly. For example, Wyatt's Rebellion lasted only eighteen days, and Essex (1601) was put down in twelve hours.

Delete as applicable

Below are a sample exam question and a paragraph written in answer to this question. Read the paragraph and decide which of the possible options (in bold) is the most appropriate. Delete the least appropriate options and complete the paragraph by justifying your selection.

'1549 was the most important turning point in the nature of unrest in the period from 1485 to 1603.' How far do you agree?

To a **great/fair/limited** extent 1549 was the most important turning point in the nature of Tudor rebellions from 1485 to 1603. **Most/some/few** rebellions in the period before 1549 lasted a few months. This was particularly noticeable with the Pilgrimage of Grace which lasted two months and was similar to the major disturbances of Kett's and the Western Rebellion in 1549. The Oxfordshire Rising of 1596 and Essex Rebellion in 1601 were **much longer/much shorter** in length. However, Irish rebellions which became more frequent in the period after 1549 **support/ challenge** this view as they sometimes lasted for a number of years. In this way, to a **great/fair/ limited** extent 1549 was the most important turning point in the nature of Tudor rebellions from 1485 to 1603 because . . .

_____

_____

 Turning assertion into argument

Below are a sample question and a series of assertions. Read the exam question and then add a justification to each of the assertions to turn each one into an argument.

Assess the reasons why the frequency of rebellion declined in the second half of the period.

During the first half of the period the Tudor monarchy had been challenged by the Yorkists, but in the second half of the period this threat had been removed because

_____

_____

During the period after 1536 religious changes had caused unrest but after 1559 this declined because

_____

_____

Also, the increased use of Parliament meant that unrest was reduced because

_____

_____

Leadership and support: nobility

> For a description of all the rebellions mentioned see pages 4–5.

Leadership and support

Leadership helped to determine the chances of success of an uprising and the threat it posed. Rebellions led by claimants to the throne or nobles were a threat to the monarchy. Although large-scale rebellions could present a challenge to the authorities, the nature of the support also affected the seriousness of the threat.

Royal claimants

Royal claimants made a rebellion more serious for the monarch, particularly when the monarch's legitimacy was dubious. Hence Simnel's claim to be Earl of Warwick (1486–87) and Warbeck's to be the Duke of York (1491–99) made Henry VII's position vulnerable because they had a stronger claim to the throne than he did. However, Mary Tudor's legitimacy meant that Northumberland was unlikely to succeed in 1553.

Nobility

Leadership by the nobility was particularly important in Ireland where nobles were heads of clans and could therefore mobilise large numbers. Noble leadership also helped to give the rebellion legitimacy and authority. The Cornish Rebellion (1497) got Lord Audley to lead the tax protest and the Pilgrimage of Grace (1536–37) besieged Pontefract Castle to persuade Lord Darcy to join. Sometimes nobles claimed they had been pressurised or threatened to lead the rebel armies, but given the likely punishments after defeat this claim was not surprising.

Although the nobility were supposed to be the monarch's agents in the localities, many rebellions attracted noble support. This was dangerous because they had finances, access to weapons and could gather their tenants to increase the numbers involved.

Noble involvement was present throughout the period (see table below).

Date	Rebellion	Noble involvement
1486	Lovel and Stafford	Francis Viscount Lovel and Humphrey and Thomas Stafford
1497	Cornish	Lord Audley
1491–97	Warbeck	Lord Fitzwater, Sir William Stanley
1536–37	Pilgrimage of Grace	Lords Hussey, Darcy, Lumley and Latimer
1553	Northumberland's **coup** – Lady Jane Grey	Earl of Oxford, Earl of Huntingdon
1554	Wyatt	Duke of Suffolk
1569	Northern Earls	Earls of Northumberland and Westmorland
1601	Essex	Earls of Essex, Southampton, Sussex, Rutland and Lords **Cromwell**, Mounteagle, Sandes

It was Essex's rebellion which attracted most noble support. However, it should also be remembered that in most rebellions the monarch was also able to raise noble support. In the rebellion of the Northern Earls, Hunsdon, Huntingdon and Sussex were able to raise troops, the Duke of Norfolk was sent to stop the Pilgrimage of Grace and Mary Tudor was able to rely on most of the nobility to help her defeat Northumberland.

Below is a sample exam question which asks how far you agree with a specific statement. Below this are a series of general statements that are relevant to the question. Using your own knowledge and information from earlier in the book, the opposite page and page 30, decide whether these statements support or challenge the statement in the question and tick the appropriate box.

'Rebellions led by members of the nobility were the most serious threat to the monarchy.' How far do you agree?

	SUPPORT	CHALLENGE
Henry VII was forced into battle at East Stoke.		
The Cornish rebels reached Blackheath.		
Yorkist challenges remained throughout Henry VII's reign.		
The protests against the Amicable Grant came from the peasantry.		
The Pilgrims wanted Lord Darcy to lead the rising.		
Robert Kett was a yeoman.		
Robert Welch may have been the leader of the Western Rising.		
Northumberland removed Mary Tudor.		
Thomas Wyatt was a member of the Kentish gentry.		
The Northern Earls raised only 5000 men.		
Essex's rebellion lasted only twelve hours.		

Complete the paragraph (a)

Below are a sample exam question and a paragraph written in answer to this question. The paragraph lacks a clear point at the start but does contain supporting material and an explanatory link back to the question at the end. Complete the paragraph by writing in the key point at the start. Use the space provided.

'The nobility became less involved in rebellion as the period progressed.' How far do you agree with this view?

_____

_____

This point is supported by the fact that during the reign of Elizabeth individual nobles such as Westmorland, Northumberland and Essex led rebellions against the monarch. These nobles felt they were losing power and had little to lose; the Northern Earls had lost control of the wardenships of the Marches and Essex had lost his monopoly over sweet wine. Although they were able to attract support from some other nobles such as Southampton and Rutland, they were not able to attract popular support, with the Northern Earls raising only 5000 men. In comparison, the government was able to rely on the support of most of the nobility. In the rebellion of the Northern Earls, Hunsdon, Huntingdon and Sussex were able to raise troops, which forced the Northern Earls to flee, and this can be contrasted with the Pilgrimage of Grace earlier in the period. Although there was something of a change in the number of nobles involved in rebellion and the scale of those risings, the later period still witnessed noble unrest.

Leadership and support: gentry

> For a description of all the rebellions mentioned see pages 4–5.

Those in the **gentry** class or just below it, **yeomen**, often provided the leadership. They had organisational experience through holding local offices and were influential in local society.

As with the nobility, gentry leadership gave the rising some legitimacy. Gentry leadership became more common in the middle period as nobles, unless they were seriously disaffected, were unwilling to risk their positions.

Date	Rebellion	Led by	Position
1489	Yorkshire	Sir John Egremont	An illegitimate member of the Percy family
1536–37	Pilgrimage of Grace	Sir Robert Aske	Lawyer, attorney to the Earl of Northumberland
1549	Western Rebellion	Sir Humphrey Arundell, John Winslade and John Bury	All quite substantial landowners in either Cornwall or Devon
1554	Wyatt	Sir Thomas Wyatt, but also Sir James Croft and Sir Peter Carew	Wyatt was a courtier and former **sheriff**, Croft held a variety of government posts and Carew was a courtier and had been High Sheriff of Devon and helped to put down the Western Rebellion

Clergy

Members of the clergy rarely led a revolt, as it was seen as a sin, but when the Catholic faith was under attack they did sometimes assume leadership roles. In the Pilgrimage of Grace, the abbots of local monasteries were involved. In the Western Rebellion, some Cornish vicars marched to Exeter and the vicar of St Thomas Exeter, Robert Welch, may have been the leader of the rising. It was a priest, Richard Symonds, who first noticed Simnel's resemblance to Richard of York and initially encouraged the conspiracy.

Commoners

Few rebellions were led by commoners. They had little local influence and were unable to raise large-scale support, as was seen in Oxfordshire in 1596. However, the Amicable Grant Rising in 1525 was led by commoners and was successful because they had sympathy in the King's Council. Much of the unrest in 1549 was led by commoners, particularly Kett in East Anglia but also many of the lesser disturbances in the South and Midlands.

Commoners were most likely to be involved in protests against government policies, notably taxation and religion (such as the Cornish Rebellion of 1497 or the Pilgrimage of Grace in 1536–37). It was their involvement that ensured the rebellion raised large numbers.

Cross-class support

Some rebellions attracted support from across the whole social spectrum. This was seen in the Cornish Rebellion, which was led by a noble but attracted mass support, and in the Pilgrimage of Grace, which had support from all classes. However, some rebellions, such as Kett's, did not attract noble or gentry support because they were about low politics.

Foreign support

Foreign support was evident in the early dynastic rebellions, with Margaret of Burgundy funding mercenaries for the Simnel Rebellion. Later rebels hoped to gain foreign support, but it never materialised:

- Pilgrimage of Grace (1536–37) – Hoped for support from Charles V.
- Wyatt (1554) – Hoped for support from France.
- Northern Earls (1569) – Hoped for papal and Spanish support.

Simple essay style

Below is a sample exam question. Use your own knowledge, information on the opposite page and information from other sections of the book to produce a plan for this question. Choose four general points, and provide three pieces of specific information to support each general point. Once you have planned your essay, write the introduction and conclusion for the essay. The introduction should list the points to be discussed in the essay and outline the line of argument you intend to take. The conclusion should summarise the key points and justify which point was the most important.

Assess the view that rebellions with cross-class support were the most threatening to the government in the period from 1485 to 1603.

Identify an argument

Below are a series of definitions, a sample exam question and two sample paragraphs. One of the paragraphs achieves a high level because it contains an argument. The other achieves a lower level because it contains only description and assertion. Using information from earlier in the book and the opposite page identify which is which. The mark scheme on page 3 will help you.

- **Description:** a detailed account
- **Assertion:** a statement of fact or an opinion which is not supported by a reason
- **Reason:** a statement that explains or justifies something
- **Argument:** an assertion justified with a reason

'The gentry were the most successful leaders of rebellion in the period from 1485 to 1603.' How far do you agree?

Sample 1

The gentry were involved in the leadership of a number of rebellions. Robert Aske, a Yorkshire lawyer, led the Pilgrimage of Grace and was able to get large numbers to rise up in support. He was also able to get the support of some important nobles such as Lords Hussey and Darcy. He was able to lead his troops to take York, the regional capital, and then seize Pontefract Castle. Therefore, Aske shows that gentry leadership was often successful.

Sample 2

There were occasions when gentry leadership was successful, at least in achieving some of the objectives of the rebellion. Robert Aske was able to raise a large force of 40,000 men which outnumbered royal forces and therefore seized the important city of York and the strategically important castle at Pontefract. Similarly, Thomas Wyatt was able to raise support from his local area around Maidstone, in Kent, and lead the rebel forces to the gates of the city of London before being defeated. Therefore, the rebellions led by the gentry were successful in achieving at least some of their initial objectives.

Objectives

For a description of all the rebellions mentioned see pages 4–5.

The Tudor rebels usually had one of three main objectives:

- to remove the monarch (dynastic rebellions)
- to force the government to change its policies – in areas such as taxation or religion
- to remove English rule from Ireland and establish independence (Irish rebellions).

Dynastic rebellions

At the start of the period it was clear that the Yorkist rebellions of 1486, 1487 and 1497 had the objective of removing Henry VII from the throne. The removal of the monarch was also evident in the plot surrounding the **Devise** in 1553, when Northumberland wanted to prevent Mary Tudor from acceding to the throne. However, other dynastic rebellions were less open in their objectives and often claimed that their aim was not to remove the monarch. This was certainly the case with:

- Wyatt (1554), who claimed he wanted to stop Mary's marriage to Philip
- the Northern Earls (1569), who wanted to force Elizabeth to name Mary Queen of Scots as heir
- Essex (1601), who wanted to remove the **Cecil faction**.

However, the aims of these last three rebellions may have concealed an ultimate aim to overthrow the monarch.

Change in government policies

Many of the rebellions were protests against government policies, particularly those relating to taxation and religious change.

Taxation

Tax rebellions often followed innovative practices, such as the introduction of taxes to fund wars, as in 1489, 1497 and 1525. The rebels wanted the government to stop the collection of the taxes.

Religious policies

Protests about religious changes usually followed legislation that had a significant impact on people's daily lives. The Pilgrimage of Grace (1536–37) followed the dissolution of the smaller monasteries, which the rebels wanted reversed, and also demanded the restoration of traditional practices and papal rule. The Western Rebellion (1549) followed the dissolution of the **chantries** and the introduction of a new, Protestant, **Prayer Book**. The rebels saw this as an attack on traditional religion and wanted the changes reversed. Similarly, the rebels in 1569 wanted an end to the religious changes introduced by Elizabeth and her bishop in Durham, Pilkington.

Social and economic policies

There were also protests about social and economic policies. Kett's rebels (1549) wanted the government to enforce anti-enclosure legislation and protect **common land**. The Western rebels (1549) wanted the government to abandon the **Sheep and Cloth tax**. In the Oxfordshire Rising of 1596, it is likely the rebels wanted the government to take action against high food prices.

Ireland

At first Irish rebellions had similar objectives to some of the English rebellions; they wanted an end to recent government political, religious and economic policies. However, by the end of the period the Irish wanted to remove the English administration and, similar to the Northern Earls, also preserve the Catholic faith.

Spot the mistake

Below are a sample exam question and a paragraph written in answer to this question. Why does this paragraph not get into Level II. Once you have identified the mistake, rewrite the paragraph so that it displays the qualities of Level II. The mark scheme on page 3 will help you.

How far did the objectives of Tudor rebellions remain the same throughout the period?

The objectives of Tudor rebellions remained the same throughout the period. The rebels usually wanted the government to change its policies. This was particularly true of religiously motivated rebellions. The Pilgrims wanted the government to end the closure of the monasteries and restore the authority of the Pope. In the Western Rebellion the rebels wanted a reversal of policy as they wanted the new Prayer Book abandoned, although there was no call for the restoration of the Pope.

 Eliminate irrelevance

Below are a sample exam question and a paragraph written in answer to this question. Read the paragraph and, using information from the page opposite and earlier in the book, identify parts of the paragraph that are not directly relevant to the question. Draw a line through the information that is irrelevant and justify your deletions in the margin.

'The reversal of government policies was the most common objective of Tudor rebellions in the period from 1485 to 1603.' How far do you agree?

Many Tudor rebellions wanted to reverse government policies. This was particularly true of religiously motivated rebellions where the rebels wanted to stop religious innovation, such as in the Pilgrimage of Grace where they wanted to preserve traditional religious institutions, such as monasteries. Monasteries were often the places where local people worshipped or provided employment, therefore the rebels restored some of the smaller monasteries in Lancashire. This was similar in the Western Rebellion which was caused by the introduction of the new Prayer Book. There had been religious tensions in Cornwall before this and therefore further religious protest was not surprising. Similarly, the rebels in the rebellion of the Northern Earls were concerned by the establishment of a Protestant regime in the North, but they also drew up a plan to marry the Duke of Norfolk to Mary Queen of Scots. However, in contrast, Kett's rebels wanted to increase the moves of Somerset's government towards Protestantism and wanted the government to ensure priests were resident and could teach the people.

Strategy, tactics and organisation

For a description of all the rebellions mentioned see pages 4–5.

Strategy and tactics

The strategy and tactics deployed by rebels depended upon their objectives.

Dynastic rebellions

Rebellions that aimed to overthrow the monarch needed to raise a large army, force the monarch into battle and have an alternative ruler available:

- Northumberland supported the claim of Lady Jane Grey (1553).
- Wyatt supported Elizabeth (1554).
- The Northern Earls supported Mary Queen of Scots (1569).
- Essex supported James VI (1601).

Simnel (1486–87) and Warbeck (1491–99) landed in remote areas and hoped to gain support from disaffected counties as they marched towards London. Both Wyatt's and Essex's rebellions began near London to try and seize the capital quickly.

Change in government policies

Rebellions where the objective was to pressurise the government into changing policies used a range of tactics:

- They tried to raise as much support as possible, particularly the support of nobles and gentry who would bring their tenants with them. For example, the Pilgrims (1536) besieged Lord Darcy in his castle at Pontefract to get his support.
- They drew up a series of grievances containing their demands, for example, the Pilgrimage of Grace (1536), the Western Rebellion (1549) and Kett's Rebellion (1549) all drew up **Articles**.
- They threatened or intimidated local gentry:
  - The Pilgrims threatened Lord Darcy, Marmaduke Neville and Sir Roger Cholmeley.
  - The Western rebels imprisoned gentry on St Michael's Mount.
  - Kett's rebels imprisoned gentry such as Sir Roger Woodhouse, Thomas Gawdy and Richard Catlyn.
- They used violence:
  - The Yorkshire rebels (1489) murdered the Earl of Northumberland as he tried to collect taxes.
  - William Hellyons was murdered by the Western rebels (1549) who also shouted 'Kill the Gentlemen'.

- They besieged regional capitals and county towns:
  - The Cornish (1497) and Western rebels besieged Exeter.
  - Kett's rebels took Norwich.
  - The Pilgrims entered York and Durham.
  - Durham was entered again by the Northern Earls.

Irish rebellions

The rebels usually avoided military confrontation and conducted a campaign that was similar to modern **guerrilla warfare**. They attacked officials in order to try and disrupt government. If defeated they often disappeared into remote areas which the English forces did not know and would not enter.

Organisation

Organisation was vital in holding a rebellion together, but some rebellions were better organised than others. The best examples of well-organised rebellions were:

- The Pilgrimage of Grace – Aske was able to control 40,000 rebels from a range of social classes. The army was organised into **hosts** based on regions. The leaders of the hosts met to discuss tactics, and pledging an oath helped ensure good discipline.
- Kett's Rebellion – Kett controlled 16,000 rebels at the camp on Mousehold Heath. His aim was to show how local government could be run effectively. **Warrants** were issued for supplies, negotiations were undertaken with the Mayor of Norwich to buy supplies and prayers were said twice a day.

Poorly organised rebellions included:

- The Rebellion of the Northern Earls – this was poorly planned as the Earls had been reluctant to rebel. Moreover, their information gathering was poor as they were unaware that Mary Queen of Scots had been moved south.
- Simnel Rebellion – Simnel's chances were lessened by the behaviour of the **mercenaries** who often pillaged and stole, which dissuaded locals from joining.
- Essex Rebellion – this lacked surprise as Essex gave notice of some action by having Shakespeare's **Richard II** performed the night before. The play culminates with the overthrow of Richard, suggesting the potential overthrow of the monarch.

Delete as applicable

Below are a sample exam question and a paragraph written in answer to this question. Read the paragraph and decide which of the possible options (in bold) is most appropriate. Delete the least appropriate options and complete the paragraph by justifying your selection.

Assess the view that Tudor rebellions were badly organised.

Most/some/no Tudor rebellions were badly organised. For example, the leadership of the rebellion of the Northern Earls was similar to that of all rebellions to a **limited/fair/great** extent in that it lacked commitment from the rebels and was poorly informed. In contrast, Aske was similar to **all/some/few** of the other rebel leaders in ensuring that the Pilgrim rebels did not disperse and that order was maintained within the forces assembled. In Kett's Rebellion he was able to exert a **limited/reasonable/considerable** degree of control through the issuing of warrants. In conclusion, the examples of the Northern Earls, Aske and Kett show that organisation of Tudor rebellions was **often/sometimes/never** poor in the sense that...

_____

_____

RAG – Rate the timeline

Below are a sample exam question and a timeline. Read the question, study the timeline and, using information from the opposite page and earlier in the book, use three coloured pens to put a Red, Amber or Green star next to the events to show:

- **Red:** Events and policies that have no relevance to the question
- **Amber:** Events and policies that have some significance to the question
- **Green:** Events and policies that are directly relevant to the question

1. 'Most Tudor rebellions wanted to avoid a battle with government forces.' How far do you agree?

Now repeat the activity with the following questions.

2. 'The tactics of rebels in the period from 1485 to 1603 remained the same.' How far do you agree?

3. To what extent were Tudor rebellions poorly organised?

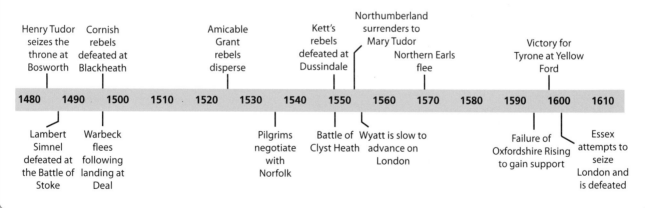

Differences between rebellions in England and Ireland

> For a description of all the rebellions mentioned see pages 4–5.

Duration and scale

Irish rebellions usually lasted much longer than English rebellions. There were a number of reasons for this:

- The English government was reluctant to send large forces to Ireland because of the cost.
- They were seen as less threatening because of the distance from London.
- The rebels avoided open warfare and were therefore harder to defeat.

Unlike English rebellions, the Irish unrest increased in scale as the period progressed. This meant that English forces had to increase. Sir Edward Poynings, **Lord Deputy** under Henry VII, had 400 troops but Lord Mountjoy, Deputy from 1600, needed 13,000 to defeat Tyrone (1595–1603).

Loyalty to the monarch

Most rebels claimed to be loyal to the monarch. However, Irish leaders were more likely to change sides and break truces.

- The Earl of Kildare backed Simnel (1486–87), then swore allegiance to Henry VII but failed to arrest Warbeck (1491–99) when he landed.
- The Earl of Desmond was held in the Tower of London for five years in an attempt to win his support, but it only encouraged him to take part in the Geraldine Rebellion of 1579–83.
- Hugh O'Neill had been brought up in the household of the Earl of Leicester and had helped with the defence of English **garrisons** between 1593 and 1594, but because he was not rewarded he led the Tyrone Rebellion. He signed a truce with the English in both 1596 and 1599, but used the time to build up forces to continue the rebellion.

Irish rebellions were more likely to end when the leaders were killed. However, this did not always happen as Desmond took on the leadership of the unrest after Fitzgerald's death in 1579.

Support

Unlike English rebellions, there were no popular rebellions in Ireland. All the rebellions were led by clan chiefs, who tried to get the support of their **tenants** in the same way as the Northern Earls. Unrest in Ireland was localised or regional and rebellion centred on the lands of the clan, except Tyrone's Rebellion, which was nationwide.

Causes

Unlike English rebellions, Irish rebellions were not caused by social and economic problems. There were three major causes of Irish unrest:

- imposition of direct rule from London
- the growing influence of English families
- religious changes.

Imposition of direct rule

Henry VIII ended the rule of the Irish nobility in Ireland and declared himself King in 1541. This meant the clan chiefs had to surrender their lands and have them re-granted according to English laws and renounce their customs, language and laws. They saw this as an attack on their traditional way of life.

The growing influence of English families

In Ireland, after 1534, English officials were given administrative posts that had usually been given to Irish families. This lost the Crown the support of families such as the Kildares. The problem was worsened by the plantation system, which meant that land was taken from rebels and granted to English landlords at reduced prices.

Religious changes

Although religion was a major cause of unrest in England between 1536 and 1569, in Ireland it was only a subsidiary cause or cloak, used to increase support. Clan chiefs often claimed that they were protecting the Catholic Church, but their primary concern was to protect their interests. However, the arrival of Catholic **missionary priests** after Elizabeth's **excommunication** in 1570 did encourage religious resistance and it can be seen as a feature of later rebellions.

Simple essay style

Below is a sample exam question. Use your own knowledge, information on the opposite page and information from other sections of the book to produce a plan for this question. Choose four general points, and provide three pieces of specific information to support each general point. Once you have planned your essay, write the introduction and conclusion for the essay. The introduction should list the points to be discussed in the essay and outline the line of argument you intend to take. The conclusion should summarise the key points and justify which point was the most important.

To what extent was the nature of English and Irish rebellions different?

 Similarities and differences

Use the information on the opposite page and your own knowledge to complete the following table to show the similarities and differences between English and Irish rebellions.

Factor	Similarity	Difference
Geographical location		
Numbers involved		
Aims and objectives		
Leadership		
Tactics of rebels		

Successful rebellions

> For a description of all the rebellions mentioned see pages 4–5.

Most Tudor rebels were defeated, often on the battlefield with heavy casualties, as at East Stoke (1486), Clyst (1549) and Dussindale (1549). However, not all rebellions ended in failure. Obviously those that aimed to overthrow the monarch can be seen to have failed when the monarch was not removed, but those that aimed at drawing attention to grievances are much harder to judge. There are certainly instances where the government responded to rebel demands and either made some concessions or brought in legislation to remove some of the grievances.

The Amicable Grant Rising (1525)

This was the only rebellion that ultimately achieved its main aim – the prevention of the collection of the tax. The king also reassessed the parliamentary subsidy. He had been granted four subsidies but still had two of the instalments to collect and he feared another refusal to pay.

The rebellion was successful for a number of reasons:

- The scale of support was considerable, growing from over 4000 at the start.
- There was cross-class support, not only from the large numbers of peasants opposed to the Grant, but also from some of Henry's councillors.

- There was resistance in London, which was a danger to the government.
- Henry could make concessions without losing power. However, he had to abandon his invasion of France.
- Henry was able to blame **Wolsey** for the tax and could therefore appear generous by abandoning it, thus improving his reputation.

Demonstrations and concessions

The government made concessions to some other rebellions, most notably where taxation and social and economic issues were concerned (see table).

However, most of the concessions did not address the main objectives of the rebels, particularly the responses to the Pilgrimage of Grace, Kett and Oxfordshire (see page 32 and below for further details).

Reasons for success

- Taxation rebellions were the most successful because governments were more willing to abandon attempts to raise revenue than risk further unrest.
- Where rebellions did achieve some success they were often well led, usually by gentry, lawyers or yeomen, who could provide effective leadership.
- Rebellions that had cross-class support, such as the Cornish, Amicable Grant and Pilgrimage of Grace, were more likely to achieve some of their objectives.

Date	Rebellion	Grievance	Concession
1489	Yorkshire	Northern counties did not usually contribute to war against France	Henry VII agreed not to collect the tax and the rebels were not fined.
1497	Cornish	West did not fund wars against Scotland	The Cornish did not have to pay the war tax, but were heavily fined. There was no further attempt at tax innovation.
1536	Pilgrimage of Grace	The religious changes, particularly the closure of the smaller monasteries and rumours of attacks on parish churches	The rebels were pardoned and Henry promised a parliament in the North, although this was never called. Religious changes were slowed down and the **Act of Six Articles** upheld traditional beliefs. **Entry fines** to rented land were set at the level demanded by the rebels, the 1534 **subsidy** was stopped and the **Statute of Uses** was repealed.
1549	Kett	Increased rents and loss of common land to the gentry	The Subsidy and Vagrancy Acts were repealed. The Enclosure Act restricted landlords' manorial rights over common land. Acts fixed grain prices and maintained **arable** land.
1549	Western	Introduction of new Prayer Book, but also the Sheep and Cloth tax	The Sheep and Cloth tax was abandoned.
1596	Oxfordshire	Enclosure of land in the area	Seven leading Oxfordshire landowners were prosecuted for enclosure of common land. Acts were passed against **decaying towns**. Acts were passed to maintain arable land.

Support or challenge?

Below is a sample exam question which asks how far you agree with a specific statement. Below this are a series of general statements which are relevant to the question. Using your own knowledge, the information on the opposite page and earlier in the book decide whether these statements support or challenge the statement in the question and tick the appropriate box.

'Rebellions under Henry VII and Henry VIII were more successful than those after 1547.' How far do you agree?

	SUPPORT	CHALLENGE
Simnel fought Henry VII at the Battle of Stoke.		
The Yorkshire tax rebels were not punished and the tax was not collected.		
The Cornish did not have to pay the war tax in 1497 but were heavily fined.		
Warbeck's attempted landings were a failure.		
Henry had to abandon his French campaign because of the failure to raise the Amicable Grant.		
The dissolution of the monasteries was speeded up after the Pilgrimage of Grace.		
Social and economic reforms were introduced after the 1549 unrest.		
Mary Tudor was able to regain the throne.		
Wyatt was able to reach the gates of the city of London.		
The Oxfordshire rebels were executed.		
Essex's Rebellion was defeated in twelve hours.		

 Spectrum of significance

Below is a sample exam question and a list of general points which could be used to answer the question. Use your own knowledge and the information on the page opposite and from earlier in the book to reach a judgement about the success of the rebellions in these general points to the question posed. Write the numbers on the spectrum below to indicate their relative success. Having done this, write a brief justification of your placement, explaining why some of these rebellions were more successful than others. The resulting diagram could form the basis of an essay plan.

'The rebellions that challenged government policy were the most successful rebellions.' Assess this view.

1. Rebellions that challenged the government's taxation policies
2. Rebellions that challenged the government's religious changes
3. Rebellions that wanted to change the monarch not government policies
4. Rebellions caused by faction rather than government polices
5. Rebellions caused by the government's social and economic policies
6. Rebellions caused by the government's attempts to introduce policies which centralise power

Most successful   Least successful

Why did rebellions fail?

Revised

For a description of all the rebellions mentioned see pages 4–5.

Types of rebellion

There were generally two types of rebellion: those that aimed to overthrow the monarch and those that were protesting about changes to government policy. Rebellions that threatened the very existence of the regime or major policy initiatives were suppressed by the government.

Dynastic rebellions

Dynastic rebellions failed because the government had to deal effectively with them to preserve its position. This was particularly true for Henry VII and Mary who had seized the throne from crowned rulers. Successful military action was usually taken against dynastic threats such as Simnel (1486–87), and Mary closed the gates of London to Wyatt, avoiding direct military confrontation.

Religious

Tudor rulers were largely unwilling to reverse religious changes because any concessions would have been seen as a weakness and encouraged further unrest. Indeed, the religious concessions made in 1536 after the Pilgrimage of Grace were temporary and soon reversed (see page 32).

Despite the protests, Tudor monarchs continued their religious policies:

- Henry closed the larger monasteries after the Pilgrimage of Grace and introduced the 1538 **injunctions**, which attacked saints, pilgrimages and holy days.
- Edward VI did not abandon the Prayer Book after the Western Rebellion (1549), and an even more Protestant one was introduced in 1552.
- Mary Tudor did not abandon her Catholic policies after Wyatt's Rebellion (1554) and began the persecution and burning of **heretics**.
- Elizabeth introduced **penal laws** against **Catholic recusants** after the rebellion of the Northern Earls (1569).

Support and leadership

Lack of support from the gentry and yeomen deprived rebellions of adequate leadership. The commoners lacked organisational experience, as

seen in the Oxfordshire Rising (1596), where secrecy was not maintained. A lack of support from the nobility or gentry also removed any hint of legitimacy, reducing the numbers who took part.

Government strategy and tactics

The government offered to pardon rebels, and to consider grievances if the rebels departed, which encouraged dispersal, but also ensured that the grievances were not addressed. By playing for time, the government knew rebels would run out of supplies and need to return home for the harvest or divisions would appear. The threat of a royal army would have frightened many rebels.

Military force

Despite not having a **standing army**, the government military forces were superior and defeated the rebels on every occasion they were deployed. Rebel forces usually lacked weapons, cavalry and supplies. The government could also call on foreign mercenaries, as in 1549 to suppress both Kett's and the Western Rebellions.

Rebel aims

Many rebellions were concerned with local grievances and therefore could not attract widespread support. Kett (1549) wanted to reform local government in East Anglia and the Cornish Rebellion (1497) was concerned about taxation in the West.

Failure to take London

If rebels were to defeat the government they needed to take London. When rebels did reach London the government acted quickly, as with the Cornish who were slaughtered at Blackheath, Wyatt who had the Ludgate closed to him, and Essex (1601) who was met with force.

Failure of foreign aid

Foreign aid either failed to materialise, as with the Pilgrimage of Grace or the rebellion of the Northern Earls, which had hoped for forces from Spain, or was lacking in scale, as with the attempts of the **Pretenders** under Henry VII, with Margaret of Burgundy supplying only 2000 troops for the Simnel Rebellion.

Simple essay style

Below is a sample exam question. Use your own knowledge, information on the opposite page and information from other sections of the book to produce a plan for this question. Choose four general points, and provide three pieces of specific information to support each general point. Once you have planned your essay, write the introduction and conclusion for the essay. The introduction should list the points to be discussed in the essay and outline the line of argument you intend to take. The conclusion should summarise the key points and justify which point was the most important.

'The most important reason for the failure of Tudor rebellions was the lack of support.' How far do you agree?

Introducing an argument

Below are a sample exam question, a list of key points to be made in the essay, and a simple introduction and conclusion for the essay. Read these and then, using the information on the opposite page and earlier in the book, rewrite the introduction and the conclusion in order to develop an argument.

'All Tudor rebellions ended in failure.' To what extent do you agree with this view?

Key points:
- The measurement of failure
- Causes of the rebellion – dynastic, tax, religious, social, factional
- Nature of the rebellion – protest?
- Government policies – legislation after the unrest
- The results of rebellion – retribution

Introduction

To an extent all Tudor rebellions ended in failure. The rebels were not able to change the monarch or government policies in most instances. Most rebellions ended with the deaths of the rebels. However, in some instances, the rebels were able to raise large forces and mount a challenge to the government.

Conclusion

Rebellions were both a success and a failure. They often failed to achieve their ultimate aim of removing the monarch or changing the religious policies. However, there were other ways in which they were a success. Many raised large numbers or forced the government to introduce legislation to deal with their grievances. Therefore Tudor rebellions were both a success and a failure.

Section 3: The impact of disturbances on Tudor governments

Government strategy: initial responses

> For a description of all the rebellions mentioned see pages 4–5.

Consultation

Tudor monarchs either consulted with their councillors or left their councillors and secretaries to deal with the unrest, but insisted on being kept informed.

- Henry VII consulted with **household servants** and called a **Great Council** when Simnel invaded in 1486.
- Henry VIII left **Wolsey** and **Cromwell** to deal with the rebellions.
- Mary and Elizabeth relied on their secretaries and councillors to devise a strategy.

The exception to this was the **Duke of Somerset** who, whilst acting as **Lord Protector** for Edward VI, was criticised for failing to consult the **Privy Council** when rebellion broke out in 1549.

Sometimes monarchs received conflicting advice. During Wyatt's Rebellion in 1554 some councillors suggested using imperial troops to put down the rising, whilst others suggested Mary should leave London. However, it was her decision to stay that defeated the rising as it was her speech to the crowds in London that rallied support.

Gathering information

It was important for the monarch to obtain accurate information about the nature and scale of rebellions. This was often a slow process as communication with the **peripheral** regions was difficult, so sometimes the monarch was inactive or made the wrong decisions. Throughout the period the monarchs used spies, secret agents and informers to gather information about unrest.

- Henry VII used agents to follow the Staffords and Lovel (1486). As a result the Staffords were arrested and Lovel was forced to flee.
- Henry VII had spies in European courts who kept him informed of the movements of Warbeck (1491–97).
- Elizabeth (1558–1603) used Francis Walsingham to keep her informed of potential unrest,

particularly with regard to Mary Queen of Scots. He employed over 50 agents and their success was a factor in the decline of unrest after 1570.

However, there were times when this system failed.

- When Henry VIII ordered the Earl of Derby to arrest the leaders of the Pilgrimage of Grace he was unaware that the Earl was some distance from the rebels so could not carry out his orders.
- The Duke of Somerset was unaware of the failure of **JPs** to carry out his order to persuade the Western rebels to disperse and the rebellion was able to grow in size. Ultimately a royal army had to be sent.

Government instructions

The first people expected to deal with the outbreak of unrest were JPs and **sheriffs**. If this failed, the nobility who lived in the area were instructed to restore order. The JPs and nobility met with varying degrees of success.

The Amicable Grant Rising (1525)

When the protestors threatened to march on London, the Dukes of Norfolk and Suffolk took command and successfully ended the unrest.

The Western Rebellion (1549)

The JPs were not strong enough to contain the rebellion. The government sent Sir Peter Carew, but his attitude inflamed the situation and turned a local protest into a serious rebellion.

Kett's Rebellion (1549)

The failure of the **gentry** and sheriff to deal with the unrest resulted in the sending of the **Lord Lieutenant**, but he did not have enough troops and was defeated. As a result the Duke of Northumberland was sent with reinforcements.

The Oxfordshire Rising (1596)

The Privy Council had already warned JPs of the potential for unrest because of the food shortages. Informers warned the JPs of a plot and they were able to arrest the leaders before unrest broke out.

Develop the detail

Below is a sample exam question and paragraph written in answer to this question. The paragraph contains a limited amount of detail. Annotate the paragraph to add additional detail to the answer.

'The government was always slow in responding to the outbreak of rebellion.' How far do you agree?

When the government discovered that there was trouble, talks were often held between the monarch and councillors to decide what action to take and this could delay their response to the unrest. Henry VII consulted his trusted servants or called a meeting of nobles to decide what to do; this was different to Elizabeth and Mary. However, Henry VIII also left similar problems for his ministers to deal with. Somerset on the other hand adopted a different approach. Consultation and information gathering were lengthy processes, as the government wanted to know all the details about the unrest in order to decide what action to take. There were often delays in gathering information and this made the government appear slow.

Turning assertion into argument

Below is a sample exam question and a series of assertions. Read the exam question and then add a justification to each of the assertions to turn it into an argument.

To what extent was gathering reliable information the most serious problem for the government when dealing with the outbreak of unrest?

Some Tudor governments had problems gathering information because

_____

_____

However, Henry VII's use of spies was successful because

_____

_____

Also, the significant use of spies under Elizabeth helped as it

_____

_____

Government tactics

For a description of all the rebellions mentioned see pages 4–5.

Without a standing army or police force, often little money and other priorities, the government was forced to adopt a range of approaches to dispersing rebels that did not involve raising a force and the resulting costs. They usually tried to avoid using force by doing one of the following:

Buying time

The government often took a hard line with rebels and threatened them with punishments unless they dispersed. However, this seldom worked. Wolsey threatened the rebels in the Amicable Grant (1525) and Cromwell was just as uncompromising with the Pilgrimage of Grace (1536–37). Despite this, on both occasions the size of the rebel forces compelled the government to negotiate to buy time whilst it attempted to increase its forces.

Using propaganda

The most important propaganda available was to claim that the Tudors were the legitimate rulers chosen by God; therefore any rebellion was a sin. The government also told the rebels that they were going against the natural order or Great Chain of Being (see page 72), which outlined everyone's place in society.

Edward VI's government launched a propaganda campaign against both the Western rebels and Kett's Rebellion in 1549. Thomas **Cranmer** wrote a homily on obedience, Philip Nichols criticised the Western rebel demands and John Cheke wrote *The Hurt of Sedition,* which compared the cities of Exeter and Norwich, praising the former for resisting the rebels. Preachers were sent to Kett's camp on Mousehold Heath to uphold the new **Prayer Book**.

Issuing pardons

The government offered pardons to rebels if they would return home, but also threatened serious punishments if they did not. However, the ringleaders were usually exempt from pardon.

- The Duke of Norfolk, on the instructions of Henry VIII, negotiated with the Pilgrims and offered a pardon, a parliament to resolve the problems and an end to the dissolution of the monasteries.
- The Duke of Somerset initially threatened the Western rebels with loss of land, but then offered two pardons provided the rebels submitted. If they did not, they faced martial law.

Taking pre-emptive measures

When there was rumour of unrest the government often took action before it developed. This policy was seen most clearly under Henry VII.

In dealing with the threat of Simnel (1486–87):

- A **papal bull** excommunicated rebels and was read by the clergy.
- The real Earl of Warwick was paraded to show Simnel was an impostor.
- The estates of the queen mother, Elizabeth Woodville, a **Yorkist**, were seized and she was put in a nunnery.
- Her son by a previous marriage was put in the Tower of London.

Similar action was taken to lessen the threat of Warbeck (1491–99):

- Pressure was put on foreign powers to deny him support.
- Henry investigated counties that were under suspicion of supporting Warbeck and even went to Warwickshire to inform potential troublemakers that the rebellion would be futile.
- The Earl of Desmond, who offered support for Warbeck in Ireland, was removed from office.
- Nobles, including Lord Stanley, were executed for supporting Warbeck.

Mary also took pre-emptive action to stop Wyatt's Rebellion (1554) from developing. This forced leaders of other parts of the plot to flee or avoid involvement.

Use the information on the opposite page to add detail to the spider diagram below.

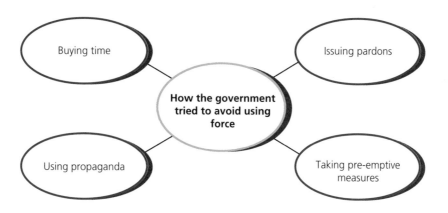

 Introducing an argument

Below are a sample exam question, a list of key points to be made in the essay, and a simple introduction and conclusion for the essay. Read these and then rewrite the introduction and the conclusion in order to develop an argument.

How successful were government tactics in dealing with the outbreak of rebellion?

Key points:

- What would be success for the government?
- How successful was buying time?
- How successful was propaganda?
- Did the rebels disperse with the issuing of pardons?
- How successful were pre-emptive measures?

Introduction

There were four key measures used by the government when rebellion broke out. The policies used included the buying of time and the use of pardons, propaganda, promises and pre-emptive measures to deal with the rebels. The success of each measure varied.

Conclusion

There were four key measures used by the government when rebellion broke out. The most successful policy was the use of pre-emptive measures. This was more successful than the other policies.

Government tactics: the use of force

> For a description of all the rebellions mentioned see pages 4–5.

Although costly, there were occasions when the government had little choice but to raise forces and combat the rebels. This was particularly true when the monarch was faced with a dynastic challenge. However, it was often the last resort, particularly in Ireland, where the terrain, poor communications and fear of increasing hostility added to the difficulties.

Raising troops

Raising troops was a slow process which explains why the government often used delaying tactics; it took six weeks for Henry VII to raise troops to face Simnel (1486–87). The government was reluctant to raise troops because of the cost and the fear that if the troops were not paid they would become more of a danger than the rebels. Also, the government relied on the nobility and gentry to raise forces and they required a licence to raise more retainers so that their forces did not become large enough to challenge the monarch.

Troop shortages

In many rebellions the rebels were able to raise more troops than the Crown.

- The Cornish rebels (1497) had a larger force than Sir Giles Daubeney, who had been in command of royal forces. The rebels were therefore able to reach Blackheath.
- In the Pilgrimage of Grace (1536–37), Robert Aske had 40,000 troops and the Duke of Norfolk who led the King's forces only 8000.
- In 1549 the Duke of Somerset faced an even greater problem. The country was at war with Scotland and there was a fear of invasion from France. At the same time, much of southern and eastern England was in revolt and he was short of money. He had to deal with smaller risings nearer to London first and that was one reason why it took so long to deal with the Western rebels and Kett.

- In the Western Rebellion (1549), Lord John Russell representing the Crown had only 300 men with him initially, but the rebel force was 6000.
- The Marquis of Northampton who led the Crown's forces had only 1500 troops to face Kett's 15,000 and was unable to prevent Kett from entering Norwich.
- In Wyatt's Rebellion (1554), the Duke of Norfolk, who led Mary's forces, was old and uninspiring. As a result, many of his troops deserted.
- Initially, in the rebellion of the Northern Earls (1569), the Earl of Sussex, President of the **Council of the North** could raise only 1000 men to fight for Elizabeth, some of whose reliability was doubtful. On the other hand, the Earls had raised 5000.

With the exception of the Pilgrimage of Grace, the government was eventually able to raise a larger force than the rebels. However, this took time and explains why the government often appeared slow to respond militarily to the outbreak of unrest.

> **The events of 1549**
>
> Over five weeks Lord John Russell was able to increase his force so that it outnumbered the Western rebels. He raised local recruits, the Earl of Wilton brought 400 troops and the Duke of Somerset diverted **mercenaries** from Scotland to join Russell.
>
> However, Kett's Rebellion was only defeated when the Duke of Northumberland arrived with 7500 troops, and this took over a month to organise.

Support or challenge?

Below is a sample exam question which asks how far you agree with a specific statement. Below this are a series of general statements that are relevant to the question. Using your own knowledge of the whole period and the information on the opposite page, decide whether these statements support or challenge the statement in the question and tick the appropriate box.

'Force was the most effective method of responding to rebellion in England.' How far do you agree?

	SUPPORT	CHALLENGE
It took Henry VII six weeks to raise a force against Simnel.		
The government was worried about the threat posed by its own forces.		
The Cornish rebels outnumbered Sir Giles Daubeney.		
The Pilgrim army outnumbered Henry VIII's by five to one.		
The Western rebels initially had a larger force than the government.		
Lord John Russell was eventually able to raise a larger force than the Western rebels.		
The Marquis of Northampton had fewer troops than Kett.		
The commander of Mary's forces against Wyatt was unable to prevent troops from deserting.		
The reliability of government forces at the start of the rebellion of the Northern Earls was doubtful.		
Over time the government was usually able to raise a larger force than the rebels.		
The gathering of royal forces was often slow because of other commitments.		

Simple essay style

Below is a sample exam question. Use your own knowledge, information on the opposite page and information from other sections of the book to produce a plan for this question. Choose four general points, and provide three pieces of specific information to support each general point. Once you have planned your essay, write the introduction and conclusion for the essay. The introduction should list the points to be discussed in the essay and outline the line of argument you intend to take. The conclusion should summarise the key points and justify which point was the most important.

How far did government methods used to combat rebellion stay the same throughout the period?

The fate of the rebels: during the rebellion

> For a description of all the rebellions mentioned see pages 4–5.

Although some rebellions ended in battle, such as Cornish (1497), Simnel (1486–87), Western (1549) and Kett's (1549), there were also many instances when the rebels avoided conflict, as with the Pilgrimage of Grace (1536–37), Wyatt (1554) and the Northern Earls (1569).

Military confrontation

The government wanted to avoid military confrontation and did not want to kill its own subjects. However, in some instances battle was necessary, such as when the rebels would not disperse or directly challenged the position of the monarch. When battles did occur the number of rebel casualties was usually very high:

- The Simnel Rebellion resulted in up to 4000 of his mercenaries being killed.
- Over 1000 Cornish rebels were killed at Blackheath.
- **Bigod's Rising** in early 1537 allowed Henry to exact revenge for the Pilgrimage of Grace and resulted in up to 700 rebels being killed as they attempted to take Carlisle.
- The battles at Clyst Heath and Sampford Courtenay reportedly killed 4000 of the Western rebels.
- The battle at Dussindale, which ended Kett's Rebellion, killed some 3000 rebels.
- Lord Dacre, a supporter of the Northern Earls, had continued to resist until 500 rebels were killed or captured at Carlisle in 1570.

Not only were large numbers killed, but many rebels were taken prisoner and faced later punishments:

- The Duke of Norfolk took more than 800 rebel prisoners at the end of the Pilgrimage of Grace.
- The Earl of Warwick entered Norwich after Kett refused a pardon and hanged rebel prisoners.

Irish rebellions

Irish rebellions resulted in few full-scale battles. There were more likely to be skirmishes, which often led to the death of the clan leader:

- Shane O'Neill was killed in a brawl with rival clans, which ended his rebellion in 1567.
- James Fitzgerald was killed during the Geraldine Rebellion of 1579–83.

However, there were also military defeats for the Irish rebels:

- Shane O'Neill's force was defeated in **Ulster** in 1567.
- Cork, which had been under siege from the rebels during the Munster Rebellion, was relieved in 1569.
- Spanish troops were defeated at Smerwick in 1580 when offering support to the Geraldine Rebellion.
- Spanish troops were defeated at Kinsale in 1601 when supporting Tyrone.

But the Irish rebels were able to inflict defeat on the English at Yellow Ford in 1598.

Avoidance of confrontation

Whether out of fear of defeat and death in battle, the lack of numbers or an unwillingness to risk the punishments that would follow military confrontation, a large number of rebellions avoided battle:

- Having landed in Cornwall in 1496, Warbeck fled rather than face Sir Giles Daubeney's army.
- Aske ordered the Pilgrims to avoid battle with the Earl of Derby's forces and keep the truce he had negotiated.
- The Duke of Northumberland backed away from military confrontation with Mary Tudor when the Earl of Oxford, the Privy Council and the government of the city of London declared for Mary over Lady Jane Grey.
- Wyatt surrendered rather than risk battle.
- The Northern Earls tried to evade the royal forces, although the Duke of Northumberland was later captured.
- The Earl of Essex (1601) avoided a battle in London.

! Delete as applicable

Below are a sample exam question and a paragraph written in answer to this question. Read the paragraph and decide which of the possible options (in bold) is most appropriate. Delete the least appropriate options and complete the paragraph by justifying your selection.

'Not all rebellions ended in battle.' Assess this view of Tudor rebellions.

It is **correct/partially correct/incorrect** to state that not all rebellions ended in battle. Dynastic rebellions often ended in battle as the rebels had to defeat the monarch in order to take the throne as was seen with the Simnel Rebellion where over 4000 of Simnel's mercenaries were killed. Popular rebellions were also **more likely/less likely** to end in battle. This view is also **correct/partially correct/incorrect** for Irish rebellions. Similarly, as the period progressed it was **more likely/less likely** for rebellion to end in battle. Consequently, it is **correct/partially correct/incorrect** to state that not all rebellion ended in battle because ...

_____

_____

_____

⚭ Identify an argument

Below are a series of definitions, a sample exam question and two sample conclusions. One of the conclusions achieves a high level because it contains an argument. The other achieves a lower level because it contains only description and assertion. Using the information on the opposite page and earlier in the book, identify which is which. The mark scheme on page 3 will help you.

- **Description:** a detailed account
- **Assertion:** a statement of fact or an opinion which is not supported by a reason
- **Reason:** a statement that explains or justifies something
- **Argument:** an assertion justified with a reason

How far did the government behave consistently in its treatment of rebel armies?

Sample 1

Throughout the period the government was consistent in its treatment of rebel forces. Although it tried to avoid confrontation, by offering pardons, as with Kett, or negotiating, as with the Pilgrims, it did engage in battle with rebel forces, particularly those who challenged the Tudor dynasty or who would not disperse. In such circumstances the government acted quite brutally and inflicted large numbers of casualties on the rebel forces: 4000 rebels were killed at Stoke in 1487 and similar numbers were also killed in 1549 in both the Western Rebellion and at Dussindale during Kett's Rebellion. Therefore, although the government tried to avoid brutal conflict, it would, when necessary, take harsh action.

Sample 2

When battles did occur the government inflicted heavy casualties on rebel forces. Henry VII killed some 4000 mercenaries and supporters of Simnel at Stoke in 1487 and the Cornish rebels also saw over 1000 killed at Blackheath. During the reign of Henry VIII large numbers were killed at the end of the Pilgrimage of Grace, following Bigod's Rising. Large numbers were also killed in 1549 at Dussindale, during the suppression of Kett's Rebellion and during the crushing of the Western Rebellion. Elizabeth I also killed large numbers of Dacre's army after the rebellion of the Northern Earls.

The fate of the rebels: after the rebellion

> For a description of all the rebellions mentioned see pages 4–5.

Trials and retribution

Punishments meted out to the rebels varied between monarchs. Henry VII and Mary Tudor were quite lenient, perhaps because their positions on the throne were not secure and they did not want to lose further support. However, Henry VIII and Elizabeth, the strongest of the rulers, were quite severe.

Henry VII (1485–1509)

Henry VII used financial penalties to punish rebels as he saw this as a way to weaken the nobility and increase royal wealth and power.

Henry VII often used **bonds and recognisances** to punish nobles, such as Lord Scrope, who were involved in rebellion. However, the ringleaders of the tax rebellions were executed. Heavy fines were also used.

Henry was initially lenient towards both Simnel and Warbeck. The former was put to work in the royal kitchens and the latter imprisoned, but both were eventually executed, accused of plotting.

Mary Tudor (1553–58)

Although Mary Tudor burnt large numbers of **heretics**, she wanted to try and win over the population after Northumberland's attempted **coup** by not treating rebels too harshly.

Initially very few of Northumberland's rebels were executed and it was only when Wyatt rebelled that Lady Jane Grey and her husband were executed. However, Mary pardoned 600 of Wyatt's rebels and executed only 71. Despite rumours of Elizabeth's links to the rebellion, Mary did not have her executed, perhaps fearing the regime would lose even more support.

Henry VIII (1509–47)

Although Henry had made promises of pardons to the Pilgrim leadership, and showed a willingness to call a parliament in the North, this was because he was outnumbered. Bigod's Rising in 1537 gave him the opportunity to go back on his word. Henry would not allow his position as Head of the Church to be challenged.

Following the Pilgrimage (1536–37), the accused in Carlisle and York were tried without a jury and a verdict without appeal was given. Monks who repossessed their monasteries were hanged. In Lancaster, the abbot of Whalley, four monks, four canons and nineteen others were executed. In total, 46 were hanged from the Lincolnshire Rising and 132 from the Pilgrimage and Bigod's Rising.

Edward VI (1547–53)

Although Edward VI was a **minor** throughout his reign, the lenient policies of his **Lord Protector**, the Duke of Somerset, towards the lower orders lost him the support of many nobles and gentry. Somerset's successor, the Duke of Northumberland, needed to regain their support and took harsh action.

After the Western Rebellion (1549) over 100 rebels were hanged in Devon and Somerset and **martial law** was imposed in Cornwall. The leading cleric Robert Welsh was hanged from his church as a sign that opposition to the religious changes was unacceptable. After Kett's Rebellion (1549) the ringleaders were executed and Kett was tortured, tried and executed.

Elizabeth I (1558–1603)

Elizabeth treated all rebels harshly. After the rebellion of the Northern Earls (1569), the Duke of Northumberland was executed and over 450 other rebels hanged. After the Oxfordshire Rising (1596) the four ringleaders were executed and others suspected of involvement were gaoled. The Earl of Essex was executed after his rising in 1601, but others were punished financially.

Irish rebellions were dealt with using martial law. Troops could therefore arrest and execute without trial anyone suspected of involvement.

- 1535–37: 70 supporters of **Silken Thomas** were hanged.
- 1569–73: 800 rebels were executed during the Munster Rebellion.
- 1580–82: The Smerwick **garrison** was massacred and other rebels hanged.
- In 1583 the head of the Earl of Desmond was sent to London for display after the unrest.

Complete the paragraph

(a)

Below are a sample exam question and a paragraph written in answer to this question. The paragraph contains a point and specific examples, but lacks a concluding explanatory link back to the question. Complete the paragraph adding this link in the space provided.

To what extent were all Tudor monarchs harsh in their treatment of rebels?

Henry VII's treatment of rebels was similar to that of Mary Tudor. Although rebels who engaged in treasonous activities knew that the penalty was death, not all rebels were put to death. As a consequence some potential rebels had bonds and recognisances imposed upon them. Mary Tudor was also lenient in her treatment of rebels after Wyatt's Rebellion, pardoning over 600 following his rebellion. However, Henry VIII, Edward VI and Elizabeth I were harsh in their treatment of rebels. After both the Pilgrimage of Grace in 1536 and the Western Rebellion of 1549 over 100 rebels were put to death, but after the rebellion of the Northern Earls in 1569 over 450 rebels were hanged and even after the minor Oxfordshire Rising of 1596, Elizabeth put all five ringleaders to death. It would therefore be fair to conclude that...

_____

_____

_____

Recommended reading

Below is a list of suggested further reading on this topic:

- *Rebellion and Disorder under the Tudors 1485–1603*, pages 80–86, Geoff Woodward (2008)
- *The Revolt of the Peasantry*, Chapters 10–13, Julian Cornwall (1977)
- *The Pilgrimage of Grace*, Chapters 16–17, Geoffrey Moorhouse (2003)

The impact of rebellion on government

Revised

> For a description of all the rebellions mentioned see pages 4–5.

The impact on the Crown

The Tudors defeated all dynastic rebellions. As the period progressed the Crown became stronger. Henry VII acted cautiously towards many rebels because of his weak claim to the throne, but Elizabeth was able to take ruthless action.

The impact on Crown servants

Crown servants were the target of many rebels:

- The Cornish rebels (1497) attacked Archbishop John Morton and Sir Reginald Bray.
- The Amicable Grant Rising (1525) attacked Cardinal Thomas Wolsey.
- The Pilgrimage of Grace (1536–37) attacked Thomas Cromwell, Thomas Cranmer and Richard Rich.
- The Northern Earls (1569) attacked William Cecil.
- The Essex Rebellion (1601) attacked Robert Cecil.

However, no minister fell directly as a result of rebellion, although Wolsey's position was weakened. Cromwell fell four years later, but this was largely due to the failure of the Cleves marriage, which was unpopular with Henry, and his advanced Protestant beliefs.

The only minister who it might be argued fell directly due to rebellion was the Duke of Somerset. However, his fall was the result of policies that favoured the lower orders, such as the **Enclosure Commission**, and his failure to suppress quickly the unrest of 1549.

The impact on foreign policy

Throughout the period, rebellion had an impact on foreign policy. It often forced a change in foreign policy as dealing with the unrest reduced the forces available to pursue foreign aims.

Henry VII (1485–1509)

The Yorkshire Rebellion (1489) occurred as Henry prepared to go to war with France over its acquisition of Brittany. The king raised a force, but the rebels fled. It did not delay the war but was a distraction for Henry. The challenge of Warbeck (1491–99) affected Henry's relations with Burgundy, France and Scotland. Henry signed the **Treaty of Etaples** with France and the **Treaty of Ayton** with Scotland to prevent their support for **Pretenders** and he put a trade embargo on Burgundy. The Cornish Rebellion (1497) impacted on preparations to attack Scotland as troops had to be diverted and this forced Henry to sign a truce with Scotland.

Henry VIII (1509–47)

Henry's reign witnessed the clearest impact of rebellion on foreign policy. The failure to raise the Amicable Grant forced Henry to abandon an invasion of France in 1525, at the very moment when France was at its weakest following the capture of **Francis I** by the **Holy Roman Emperor**.

Edward VI (1547–53)

The 1549 unrest had a serious impact on foreign policy. England had gone to war against Scotland in 1542. Following victory at Solway Moss in 1542, and a further victory at Pinkie in 1547 a decision was taken to try and conquer Scotland through a garrisoning policy. However, this policy had to be abandoned as the troops were needed to put down the rebellions. Moreover, the unrest encouraged France to declare war on England in August 1549, at the very time when troops were needed to deal with the unrest.

Mary Tudor (1553–58)

Wyatt's Rebellion (1554) encouraged anti-Spanish feeling in England and damaged Anglo-Spanish relations. In the long term this may have been a contributory factor in encouraging Spain to aid Irish rebels against England (see page 56).

The impact on domestic policy

The government did introduce some policy changes after rebellions and these are considered on pages 38 and 54.

Spot the mistake

Below are a sample exam question and a paragraph written in answer to this question. Why does this paragraph not get into Level II? Once you have identified the mistake, rewrite the paragraph so that it displays the qualities of at least Level II. The mark scheme on page 3 will help you.

To what extent did Tudor rebellions affect foreign policy?

Rebellions usually had a limited impact on Tudor foreign policy. The greatest impact was on Henry VII. He was forced to make peace with Scotland so that he could deal with the Cornwall Rebellion. Henry VII also put a trade embargo on Burgundy to stop them giving support to Perkin Warbeck. Henry VII also signed the Treaty of Etaples with France so that they did not give support to Warbeck. Therefore it can be seen that foreign policy was affected during the reign of Henry VII.

 Spectrum of significance

Below is a sample exam question and a list of general points which could be used to answer the question. Use your own knowledge and the information on the opposite page to reach a judgement about the importance of these general points to the question posed. Write the numbers on the spectrum below to indicate their relative importance. Having done this, write a brief justification of your placement, explaining why some of these factors are more important than others. The resulting diagram could form the basis of an essay plan.

'The most important impact of rebellions on Tudor governments was the overthrow of Crown servants.' How far do you agree?

1 The overthrow of the Duke of Somerset (1549)
2 The trade embargo with Burgundy
3 The Treaties of Ayton and Etaples
4 The fall of Cardinal Wolsey and Thomas Cromwell
5 The abandonment of the garrison policy in Scotland (1549)
6 The abandonment of the invasion of France (1525)

Most important   Least important

The impact of rebellion on society

> For a description of all the rebellions mentioned see pages 4–5.

Government response to the immediate aftermath of rebellion was often harsh, but there was also some willingness to remedy the rebels' grievances.

Religious policy

Tudor governments did not abandon their religious policies as a result of unrest. It may even be argued that rebellion speeded up religious changes (see page 40). The rebellion of the Northern Earls was followed by **penal laws** against Catholics who did not attend church.

Taxation

Policy was often modified. For example:

- Taxes were not collected after either the Yorkshire (1489) or Cornish Rebellion (1497).
- The Amicable Grant was abandoned at the end of May 1525.

Social and economic policies

Changes to social and economic policies were most noticeable after 1549 and in the 1590s because the government wanted to claim that the causes of unrest, particularly in 1549, were social and economic rather than religious, and that they could claim they were taking action to deal with the problems.

There was a concern after the 1549 unrest to restore order. This was done by the passing of an 'Act for the Punishment and Rising of the King's subjects' and Lord Lieutenants were given control of **county levies**, and were given training, which made them more efficient. This was followed by a series of measures designed to alleviate the social and economic problems as the government feared that rising prices and unemployment had fuelled the unrest:

- 1551: revaluation of the coinage – this helped to stop the fall in the purchasing power of the coinage and therefore helped to lessen the rise in prices that had made labourers worse off.
- 1552: limit on the conversion of **arable** land to pasture – this discouraged **enclosure**, which had

been a cause of unrest in 1549 as fewer labourers were needed.

- 1552: corn dealers were licensed – this helped to control the price of corn.
- 1552: systematic collection and disbursal of alms – this helped provide aid to those in poverty.
- 1552–55: measures to regulate the cloth industry – the cloth industry was a major employer and a lack of regulation had resulted in falling standards and a decline in sales, causing unemployment.

Similar measures followed the unrest caused by food shortages and the Oxfordshire Rising in 1596 (see pages 18–19).

The impact on regions

The North

Rebellion gave the Crown the opportunity to increase its control over the North and this can be seen after both the Pilgrimage of Grace (1536–37) and the rebellion of the Northern Earls (1569).

After the Pilgrimage of Grace:

- The Council of the North was reformed with lesser gentry given roles, whilst Henry assumed overall responsibility for the marcher lands.
- Lesser gentry were appointed under Henry VIII as deputy wardens of the border lands.
- JPs were changed and those who had shown sympathy with the rebels were removed.
- Henry VIII visited York.

After the rebellion of the Northern Earls:

- Men without local connections, such as the Earl of Huntingdon, were brought in to run the Council.
- **Magistrates** who had Catholic sympathies were purged and replaced with Protestants.

Ireland

Although rebellion in Ireland was caused by changes in policy, it also encouraged further change. Some of the major Irish families, such as the Geraldines and Kildares, were replaced by English officials. Land was redistributed, the beneficiaries being English settlers. Land was also taken from monasteries and bishops to pay for the cost of putting down the unrest.

Simple essay style

Below is a sample exam question. Use your own knowledge, information on the opposite page and information from other sections of the book to produce a plan for this question. Choose four general points, and provide three pieces of specific information to support each general point. Once you have planned your essay, write the introduction and conclusion for the essay. The introduction should list the points to be discussed in the essay and outline the line of argument you intend to take. The conclusion should summarise the key points and justify which point was the most important.

'The losses outweighed the gains.' Assess this view of the impact of Tudor rebellions on society.

Develop the detail

Below is a sample exam question and a paragraph written in answer to this question. The paragraph contains a limited amount of detail. Annotate the paragraph to add additional detail to the answer.

How far was royal authority strengthened as a result of rebellion?

Perhaps the most notable area where royal authority was strengthened in response to rebellion was in the peripheral counties of the North. The North was a dangerous area for the Tudors. This was clearly seen in the reigns of both Henry VIII and Elizabeth I who took action to improve royal control after the Pilgrimage of Grace and the rebellion of the Northern Earls. The monarchs were concerned to bring in men whom they could trust and remove those who were less reliable, even if they had not been involved in unrest, and this was done in a number of areas of local government. This often meant that men of a lower social status, who owed their power to the monarch, were brought in to replace those who had influence in the area. Some monarchs went even further and visited the North, but this was not a regular occurrence.

The threat of rebellion to Tudor governments

For a description of all the rebellions mentioned see pages 4–5.

Factors that increased the threat of rebellions

The size and nature of support

If the number of rebels was larger than the number in the government forces, this increased the threat. This was the case, at least initially, with:

- the Cornish Rebellion (1497)
- the Amicable Grant Rising (1525)
- the Pilgrimage of Grace (1536–37)
- Kett's Rebellion (1549)
- the Western Rebellion (1549)
- the rebellion of the Northern Earls (1569).

The rebellion was more threatening if it acquired foreign and noble support. This was the case with:

- the Simnel Rebellion (1486–87)
- Warbeck's Rebellion (1491–99)
- the Pilgrimage of Grace (1536–37).

The threat was further increased if the rebels were able to force the king into battle, as happened with Simnel. This threat was made greater as Henry VII had only just come to the throne and was uncertain of noble support. Sometimes foreign powers were able to supply mercenaries or soldiers to fight for the rebels.

The aim of the rebellion

Rebellions that aimed to overthrow the monarch were the most serious threat. Thus the following rebellions constituted a direct challenge to the Tudors:

- the Simnel Rebellion (1486–87)
- Warbeck's Rebellion (1491–97)
- Lady Jane Grey (1553)
- Wyatt's Rebellion (1554)
- the rebellion of the Northern Earls (1569)
- the Essex Rebellion (1601).

Location

Rebellions that were close to, entered or occurred within London were also a greater threat as their location would make it easier to remove the government. However, London remained loyal throughout the period, even when rebels entered the city. For example, Mary was able to rally the city against Wyatt. The city had also supported her against the Duke of Northumberland's attempt to put Lady Jane Grey on the throne a year earlier.

Factors that lessened the threat of rebellions

Government tactics

In many instances, such as the Pilgrimage of Grace, the government offered concessions to the rebels, but had no intention of keeping them once the unrest had died down. However, many rebels believed that their grievances would be resolved. The offer of pardons that accompanied most rebellions encouraged some rebels to disperse, whilst propaganda may have weakened their cause. When the government was able to delay rebel activity, many rebels returned home to tend their crops.

Nature of the unrest

Most of the rebellions in the period were localised protests against local grievances or government policies. They had no intention of overthrowing the government, but wanted concessions or a change in policy. Sometimes, as with tax rebellions, the government was able to grant this, which lessened the threat.

Government support

Throughout the period the government was able to maintain the support of the majority of clergy and nobility. The clergy were used to preach against rebellion, whilst the lack of noble support deprived the rebels of legitimacy and leadership.

However, Irish rebellions were different and were a serious problem. The government lacked a large force in Ireland to crush the unrest. Irish nobles and clergy were often opposed to the government and the rebels had the advantage of knowing the land. Towards the end of the period the rebels were able to gain Spanish support. As a result, the rebellions were often lengthy and costly affairs, but even in Ireland the government emerged victorious.

Below are a sample exam question and a timeline. Read the question, study the timeline and, using information from the opposite page and earlier in the book, use three coloured pens to put a Red, Amber or Green star next to the events to show:

- **Red:** Events and policies that have no relevance to the question
- **Amber:** Events and policies that have some significance to the question
- **Green:** Events and policies that are directly relevant to the question

1) To what extent were dynastic rebellions a threat to Tudor governments?

Now repeat the activity with the following questions.

2) 'Rebellions with foreign support were a great threat to Tudor governments.' How far do you agree?

3) To what extent were the rebellions in peripheral regions a serious threat to Tudor governments?

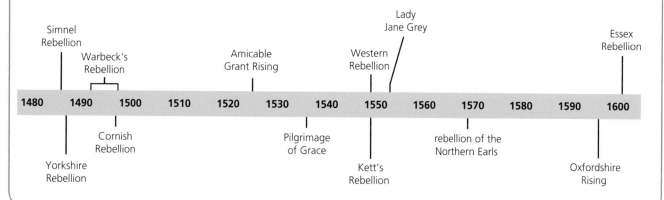

Below is a sample question and a series of assertions. Read the exam question and then add a justification to each of the assertions to turn it into an argument.

'Tudor governments were never seriously threatened by rebellion.' How far do you agree?

Rebellions were a threat to Tudor governments in so far as some rebellions were able to

_____

_____

However, it was dynastic rebellions that were the greatest threat because

_____

_____

Moreover, foreign support made these challenges greater because

_____

_____

Section 4: The maintenance of political stability

The role of the Crown

Revised

For a description of all the rebellions mentioned see pages 4–5.

Although there was minor unrest and a significant number of rebellions, disorder was still the exception. When faced with challenges to its authority the government brought in short-term measures. Moreover, the monarchy was able to develop institutions and policies that resulted in the decline of rebellion. This section will look at the role of the central and local authorities in attempting to maintain stability.

The monarchy was the most important agent in the maintenance of stability. The monarch had ultimate authority, as he or she was believed to be appointed by God. Any rebellion against the monarch was seen as a sin against God. The monarch's authority was increased after the **Reformation** and Henry VIII's break with Rome, when subjects no longer held obedience to the Pope in spiritual matters, only to God and the King.

The hierarchical nature of society reinforced the belief in obedience to the ruler. This was increasingly upheld through Tudor propaganda. Writers such as Richard Hooker and Edmund Dudley argued that everyone had a place in society and should accept it. The development of the printing press allowed such messages to be disseminated to a wide, increasingly literate, audience.

How did Tudor monarchs reinforce their authority?

- Office holders had to swear oaths of allegiance.
- Individuals and institutions swore **oaths of succession and supremacy**.
- Monarchs issued proclamations which were read out in churches and market places.
- Propaganda was used.
- Patronage was used.

Propaganda

It is difficult to know how effective propaganda was, but all monarchs used it to a varying degree. Henry VII developed the image of the Tudor rose, which showed the unity of the houses of York and Lancaster and claimed descent from the legendary King Arthur to bolster his claim to the throne.

Henry VIII used paintings that showed his physical presence and therefore his strength and power. This image was repeated on coins. He also built lavish palaces, such as Nonsuch, to reflect his authority.

It was much harder for Edward, as a young boy, and Mary, as a female ruler who could not be shown in military dress, to portray their power. However, Edward's image did appear on coins and became more militaristic as his reign progressed, signifying his increasing authority and power.

Yet it was Elizabeth who made the greatest use of propaganda. She toured much of southern and central England during many summers, undertaking **royal progresses** and staying with leading nobles and **gentry** so that she was seen by the people, reinforcing loyalty. Pageants were held frequently which depicted her as the instrument of stability and the saviour of the nation. Paintings were used to show her wisdom and leadership, particularly after the defeat of the **Armada**. She was also represented as the goddess Astraea, a mythical woman renowned for her beauty, giving the impression that Elizabeth was her equivalent.

Patronage

All Tudor monarchs used rewards to keep the political elite subservient. Henry VII created the Order of the Garter, which was used as the ultimate sign of honour by the king. Monarchs also used **peerages** and knighthoods, **grants of monopolies** and land to reward loyal servants. The possibility of gaining rewards attracted many to court and encouraged loyalty, providing the rewards were not dominated by one **faction**, as happened under Elizabeth when she bestowed numerous rewards on the Cecil family, sparking the Earl of Essex to rebel. Retaining the loyalty of the nobility was particularly important as monarchs had no army of their own and relied on nobles raising troops to put down unrest.

Identify an argument

Below are a series of definitions, a sample exam question and two sample conclusions. One of the conclusions achieves a high level because it contains an argument. The other achieves a lower level because it contains only description and assertion. Identify which is which. The mark scheme on page 3 will help you.

- **Description:** a detailed account
- **Assertion:** a statement of fact or opinion, which is not supported by a reason
- **Reason:** a statement that explains or justifies something
- **Argument:** an assertion justified with a reason

How far do you agree that all Tudor monarchs were successful in reinforcing their authority?

Sample 1

Although all Tudor monarchs attempted to reinforce their authority, some were more successful than others. It was particularly difficult for Edward VI and Mary Tudor to accomplish this. However, the other monarchs were more successful and were able to use a variety of methods to achieve it. Royal authority was often reinforced by the use of propaganda and patronage. Monarchs went on royal progresses round the country and this helped to reinforce their image, as did the building of royal palaces or their portrayal in works of art. Tudor monarchs also gave out a variety of rewards, either titles or land, in order to keep the support of the nobility.

Sample 2

Although all Tudor monarchs attempted to reinforce their authority, some were more successful than others. The most successful were Henry VIII and Elizabeth I, who not only made their subjects swear oaths to the Acts of Succession and Supremacy, but also made use of both patronage and propaganda to maintain the loyalty of most of their subjects. Both monarchs rewarded loyal servants with grants of land and Elizabeth also issued grants of monopolies. They also ensured that they were portrayed as strong powerful rulers, either through paintings, as happened with Elizabeth after the Armada, or in military uniform for Henry VIII. However, Edward VI and Mary Tudor were less successful as neither of these monarchs could be portrayed in military splendour as Edward was a minor and Mary a female.

 Turning assertion into argument

Below is a sample question and a series of assertions. Read the exam question and then add a justification to each of the assertions to turn it into an argument.

'The institution of the monarchy was the most important element in the maintenance of stability.' How far do you agree?

The institution of the monarchy was important in the maintenance of political stability because

_____

Moreover, monarchs worked hard to enhance their respect and aura because

_____

However, they were also dependent upon the support of the nobility because

_____

The role of the Church

> For a description of all the rebellions mentioned see pages 4–5.

Throughout the period, the Church upheld the Tudor monarchy, even if some clergy and monks were involved in unrest. Despite the religious changes of the Reformation there was much continuity in the form of worship, the role of religion and even in parish clergy, which helped to create stability.

The Church had an important role in maintaining stability as it was a central influence in people's lives. It was usually the centre of the local community – carrying out baptisms, marriages and burials – as well as being the focus for most social life. Everyone was expected to attend church on Sundays. It also played an important role in supporting the Crown in national life:

- Bishops were Crown appointees, even before the Reformation.
- Bishops anointed monarchs with holy oil at the coronation.
- Clerics were used as advisors, for example William Warham and Richard Fox, who advised both Henry VII and VIII, and Cuthbert Tunstall, Thomas **Wolsey** and Rowland Lee who advised Henry VIII. Henry VIII later appointed Lee to run the Council of Wales (see page 66). However, their importance did decline under Elizabeth.
- The Church leaders supported the Crown against rebels; even the Pope threatened with **excommunication** any who fought against Henry VII at Stoke, when Lambert Simnel had invaded, or Blackheath, when the Cornish rebels reached London.

The link with the state was strengthened after the Reformation as the Church came under the Crown's **jurisdictional control** and bishops owed loyalty solely to Crown rather than to the Pope.

The parish clergy

The parish clergy played a vital role in local politics and had the power to both stabilise and destabilise the country. Attendance at church on Sunday meant that priests had the opportunity to instruct and remind people of their duties and obligations, or to encourage resistance. Clergy were encouraged to inform bishops of any rumours of trouble. The parish clergy also became important in the administration of the **Poor Law** and helped to control other social problems.

The Church and obedience

The Church could help to reinforce obedience through preaching, and sermons allowed the government to keep the country informed of its policies. In the 1530s priests were given detailed instructions on the content of their sermons and instructed to preach at least four times per year on obedience. Under Edward VI, Thomas **Cranmer** wrote a series of **homilies**, including one on obedience, which were read out during the unrest of 1549. In the 1590s bishops reminded their congregations of the government efforts to tackle social and economic problems.

Disobedience

Throughout the period the Church upheld order. However, there were times, particularly from 1530 to 1570, when the behaviour of some clergy appeared at odds with this objective.

Theories of disobedience developed during the sixteenth century when some writers argued it was God, rather than the monarch, who should be obeyed. Clergymen such as John Fisher, Hugh Latimer, Nicholas Ridley and Thomas Cranmer all adopted passive resistance: Fisher refused to acknowledge Henry VIII as Head of the Church and Latimer, Ridley and Cranmer refused to accept Mary's restoration of papal authority. These theories of resistance developed further under Mary's reign. Writers, such as John Ponet in 1556, argued that rulers had to be just and, if they acted against God, rebellion could be justified, provided it was led by a noble, **JP** or mayor. However, once the Protestant Elizabeth came to the throne these ideas declined among Protestants, although some Catholics took them up, supported by **papal sanction** after 1570.

Some clergy also encouraged social justice, with men such as Latimer arguing that obedience must be matched by the proper exercise of duty by those in authority.

Develop the detail

 a

Below is a sample exam question and paragraph written in answer to this question. The paragraph contains a limited amount of detail. Annotate the paragraph to add additional detail to the answer.

'Throughout the Tudor period the Church consistently supported the Crown.' How far do you agree?

The Church was an important institution in the maintenance of stability. At every coronation monarchs were anointed with holy oil, a clear sign of the link between the Church and state. This link continued as many Tudor monarchs used bishops as administrators and for advice. Some monarchs appointed bishops to very high office, a clear sign of their dependence on them in the government of the kingdom. This process continued for much of the period, although the second half of the period saw less use made of bishops as administrators. The Church was also able to support the monarch by threatening or actually excommunicating any who fought against the king.

 Introducing an argument

Below are a sample exam question, a list of key points to be made in the essay, and a simple introduction and conclusion for the essay. Read these and then, using the information from the page opposite and from the rest of this section, rewrite the introduction and the conclusion in order to develop an argument.

How far did the Church help to maintain stability in England in the period from 1485 to 1603?

Key points:

To answer this question you should compare and contrast the impact on stability of:

- the Church
- the monarchy
- Parliament
- Royal Councils
- the nobility
- the gentry
- the lower orders.

Introduction

To an extent the Church helped stabilise England in this period. The Church preached obedience to the monarch, with Cranmer writing a homily on obedience. The Church also threatened those who fought against Henry VII with excommunication. The break with Rome did not weaken the relationship between the Church and state as bishops were appointed by the Crown and owed their loyalty to the monarch alone. During the later period monarchs did not use clergy as political office holders.

Conclusion

The Church was important in the maintenance of stability. Monarchs often looked to clerics for advice as with Henry VII and Henry VIII who used Bishops Fox, Warham and Wolsey, all of whom helped to administer the realm. However, the Church was not the only factor in the maintenance of stability and other institutions were more important.

The role of government policies

> For a description of all the rebellions mentioned see pages 4–5.

Although governments were frequently successful in dealing with political issues, the religious and economic policies, particularly in the first half of the sixteenth century, often caused unrest.

Religious policies

The religious reforms of Henry VIII and Edward VI were a cause of conflict. Henry VIII's dissolution of smaller monasteries was a cause of the Pilgrimage of Grace (1536–37). Edward VI's dissolution of the **chantries**, and the introduction of the 1549 **Prayer Book**, helped spark the Western Rebellion.

The Elizabethan Religious Settlement, declaring Elizabeth Supreme Governor and establishing a moderate Protestantism, was most effective in creating religious stability. She established outward conformity and most Catholics accepted the Oaths of Uniformity and Supremacy. The lack of support for the Northern Earls (1569) showed the policy's success.

Economic policies

Innovative taxation caused unrest in the early Tudor period (see pages 10–11). However, after 1540 governments tried to find other ways of raising money to avoid heavy tax demands. They **debased the coinage**, sold crown lands, borrowed from overseas, cut expenditure and avoided war whenever possible. Most importantly, Elizabeth did not increase taxes in line with **inflation**. Therefore, unrest caused by financial policies declined.

Enclosure

The government was concerned to prevent **enclosure** as it caused unemployment. Commissions were established to enquire into unlawful enclosure and this encouraged people to use litigation, rather than force, to challenge enclosures. However, in 1548–49, the establishment of an **Enclosure Commission** under **Lord Protector** Somerset provoked unrest as many believed that Somerset sympathised with their concerns. They believed that by throwing down illegal enclosures they were just enacting the Commission's likely findings.

Food supplies

Many of the population lived close to starvation level and one in four harvests were poor so the government had to take action to prevent **food riots**. The lack of food riots, even in the 1580s and 1590s when harvests were particularly poor, suggests that the measures were mostly effective.

The government passed acts limiting the export of grain in 1534, 1555, 1559, 1563, 1571 and 1593. Measures were also taken to prevent its hoarding in 1527, 1544, 1545, 1550, 1556 and 1562. The government also issued JPs with Books of Orders in 1527, 1550, 1556 and 1586 on how to deal with shortages. Meanwhile, in the 1590s JPs were instructed on how to move corn to areas suffering from shortages.

Unemployment

Outside farming, the cloth trade was the largest employer and any decline in sales resulted in workers losing their jobs. Unemployment could cause unrest so the government took measures to regulate the trade and maintain the quality of cloth to sustain exports. The most notable piece of legislation was the 1563 Statute of Artificers, which fixed maximum wages and restricted the movement of all workers, as the unemployed travelling in search of work was seen as a threat to stability.

Social policies

The government was concerned with the rising number of poor and beggars, who were seen as a threat to law and order. Laws were passed, initially just punishing them. Under Elizabeth, however, acts provided for those who were sick or old. Parishes were required to provide work for the unemployed. By the 1590s, the genuine poor were assisted, but the 'undeserving' were still punished. Although it is difficult to judge the impact of this legislation, there was very little unrest in the 1590s despite the poor economic situation.

Support or challenge?

Below is a sample exam question which asks how far you agree with a specific statement. Below this are a series of general statements that are relevant to the question. Using your own knowledge, the information on the opposite page, page 64 and information from earlier in the book, decide whether these statements support or challenge the statement in the question and tick the appropriate box.

'Government policies destabilised England.' How far do you agree?

	SUPPORT	CHALLENGE
Parliament voted for Henry VII to have extra money for wars against France and Scotland (1489 and 1497)		
Statutes of 1487 and 1504 limited retaining		
Henry VII passed 138 Acts of Attainder		
Government attempt to raise Amicable Grant (1525)		
The dissolution of the smaller monasteries (1536)		
The Act of Six Articles (1539)		
The Enclosure Commission (1548)		
The new Prayer Book (1549)		
Introduction of penal laws against Catholics (1571)		
Reforms to the Council of the North after the rebellion of the Northern Earls (1569)		

 RAG – Rate the timeline

Below are a sample exam question and a timeline. Read the question, study the timeline and, using information from the opposite page, page 64 and earlier in the book, use three coloured pens to put a Red, Amber or Green star next to the events to show:

- **Red:** Events and policies that have no relevance to the question
- **Amber:** Events and policies that have some significance to the question
- **Green:** Events and policies that are directly relevant to the question

1) 'Government legislation was the most important factor in the maintenance of political stability.' How far do you agree?

Now repeat the activity with the following questions.

2) Assess the view that Elizabeth I's reign was the most successful in the use of legislation to increase stability.

3) To what extent did government policies create political instability in the period?

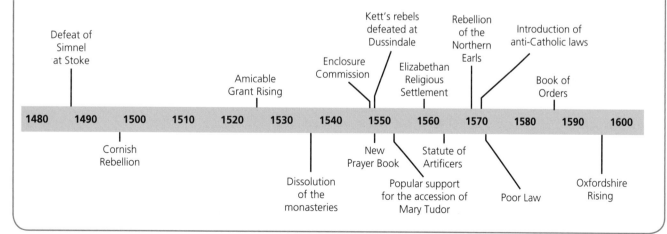

The role of Parliament

For a description of all the rebellions mentioned see pages 4–5.

Although Parliament passed many of the measures described on page 62, it must be remembered that it was not a regular part of Tudor government. For example, it met only thirteen times during Elizabeth's 46-year reign. It met only when the monarch summoned it and could also be dissolved or **prorogued** whenever the monarch desired. However, Parliament played a valuable role as a sounding board for government policy and by the end of the period membership was seen as a status symbol among the gentry.

The importance of Parliament

Although Parliament was not a permanent feature of Tudor administration, it did play an important role at various stages in the period.

- Henry VII used Parliament to help secure his rule through the Acts of Livery and Maintenance in 1487 and 1504, which clamped down on illegal retaining, which had been a cause of unrest.
- The House of Lords was a court of law and tried nobles who had been involved in rebellion, such as Lords Hussey and Darcy (1537 following the Pilgrimage of Grace), Lord Dacre (1570 after the rebellion of the Northern Earls) and the Earl of Essex (1601).
- **Acts of Attainder** were passed against rebels, with Henry VII's Parliaments passing 138 Acts.
- Religious changes were enacted by Parliament, which allowed the monarch to claim the changes had the support of the political nation.
- Parliament, rather than rebellion, was used by the nobility and gentry to express their grievances.
- Parliament provided the gentry and nobility with an opportunity to influence policy.
- Parliament voted for taxation, which early in the period caused disquiet (when taxes were raised to pay for wars against France (1489) and Scotland (1497)), but also raised essential funds for the suppression of unrest.
- Parliament passed legislation to protect the monarch; legislation was passed after 1571 to protect Elizabeth from Catholic plots and **Jesuits**.

The limitations to the use of Parliament

Parliament was not always used to increase stability. Once Henry VII was more secure he summoned Parliament only twice in his last twelve years. During Edward VI's reign, particularly in the period 1547–49, decisions were imposed using proclamations, such as punishments for vagabonds, sentencing them to two years' slavery for the first offence and life imprisonment if caught again. During Mary's reign, Parliament was critical of some policies, particularly her marriage and the war against France.

The growing importance of Parliament

At the start of the period few wanted to be MPs as it was unpaid and cost a great deal to stay in London during sessions. However, by the end of the period many gentry wanted to be MPs and wanted their sons to follow them. The government was pressurised to create more parliamentary seats to meet this increased demand. Instead of leading protests in the country, the gentry now had the opportunity to discuss high politics and, more importantly, issues that affected local law and order, such as Poor Laws and economic regulations. As a result of their involvement in discussions the gentry were less likely to lead rebellions and unrest as they had another outlet through which to air their concerns.

Spot the mistake

Below are a sample exam question and a paragraph written in answer to this question. Why does this paragraph not get into Level II? Once you have identified the mistake, rewrite the paragraph so that it displays the qualities of at least Level II. The mark scheme on page 3 will help you.

'The importance of Parliament in the maintenance of political stability increased during the period.' How far do you agree?

> Parliament was not a permanent part of the government of England and Ireland in the period. Parliament met only when the monarch wanted it and the monarch could dissolve or prorogue it at will. Although at the start of Henry's reign he used Parliament to pass Acts which limited retaining and to pass a significant number of Acts of Attainder, he summoned Parliament only twice in the last twelve years of his reign. Parliament under Elizabeth passed acts to protect her from the Catholic threat following plots and the arrival of Jesuit priests.

 Developing an argument

Below is a sample exam question, a list of key points to be made in the essay, and a paragraph from the essay. Read the question, the key points and the sample paragraph. Using the information from the page opposite and from the rest of the section, rewrite the paragraph in order to develop an argument. Your paragraph should explain why the factor discussed in the paragraph is either the most significant factor or less significant than another factor.

'Parliament played a significant role in the maintenance of political stability.' Assess this view.

Key points:

To answer this question you should compare and contrast the impact on stability of the following groups and institutions:

- Parliament
- the monarchy
- Royal Councils
- the Church
- the nobility
- the gentry
- the 'middling sort' and lower orders.

Sample paragraph

> Parliament met only when the monarch summoned it. Its most important role was in passing religious, social and economic legislation. The legislation justified the religious changes and showed that the monarch had the support of the political nation. Parliament also passed laws to try and ease food shortages in the 1590s, preventing the export of grain or ensuring through the Book of Orders that JPs had the power to distribute it where needed.

The role of councils

> For a description of all the rebellions mentioned see pages 4–5.

Councils were crucial in the government of the kingdom. At the centre was the King's Council, which became the **Privy Council** during the 1530s. There was also a series of regional councils.

Their purpose was to put the monarch's wishes into practice and enforce laws. This was important in regions that were far from London and where the king's **writ** was more difficult to enforce because of the power of local families.

The Privy Council

Under Henry VII (1485–1509) over 200 men attended council meetings, although fewer than twenty attended regularly. However, by 1540 a select group formed the Privy Council. Its development was the result of the Pilgrimage of Grace (1536–37) and Henry's need for advice. Its importance grew under Elizabeth until by the end of the period it was meeting every day. It was involved in implementing government policy such as:

■ the Religious Settlement (see page 62)
■ crushing rebellion in Ireland (see below).

The Council also carried out routine work which helped to maintain stability such as organising the work of JPs, co-ordinating defences and overseeing parliamentary elections to ensure supporters of the Crown were elected.

Regional councils

Regional councils received their orders from the Council in London, but also developed into administrative and judicial bodies.

The Council of the North

The Council of the North was a **Yorkist** creation and was dominated at the start of Henry VII's reign by Yorkist families such as the Percys. To increase his control over the region Henry VII appointed the Earl of Surrey as his chief representative on the Council. The Earl had no links to the region and needed to prove his loyalty to get his estates restored following his earlier support for the Yorkist cause.

After the Pilgrimage of Grace, the Council was remodelled as Henry VIII attempted to increase his control over the North. In 1537 the Council was given judicial functions and acted as a **Star Chamber** under the loyal Cuthbert Tunstall, Bishop of Durham.

Edward and Mary restored the power of the traditional families, but following the rebellion of the Northern Earls (1569) Elizabeth appointed her cousin and strong Protestant, the Earl of Huntingdon, as president. There was no further unrest in the region, despite the region's support for Catholicism.

The Council of Wales

The Welsh borders were less of a problem for the Tudors than the North. There were few powerful landowners. The Council was usually run by bishops such as Rowland Lee (1534–43), who restored royal power by rebuilding royal castles and enforcing justice. Although the quality of justice varied, there were no rebellions.

The Council of the West

The Council of the West was set up in 1538 to administer Cornwall, Devon, Dorset and Somerset, but lasted only two years. The reasons for its establishment are not clear; it could have been a response to:

■ the fall of the powerful Courtenay family following the **Exeter Conspiracy** of 1538 which meant there was no powerful family in the region
■ the fear of invasion from France and Spain following a truce between the two nations.

The Council did much to organise defences and there was no unrest in the region until 1549.

The Council of Ireland

The Council of Ireland was the least successful council. Only by working with local clan chiefs was stability possible. After 1534 the use of English governors to rule on the monarch's behalf created resentment as power had previously resided with Irish nobles. This led to regular rebellions.

Simple essay style

Below is a sample exam question. Use your own knowledge, information on the opposite page and information from other sections of the book to produce a plan for this question. Choose four general points, and provide three pieces of specific information to support each general point. Once you have planned your essay, write the introduction and conclusion for the essay. The introduction should list the points to be discussed in the essay and outline the line of argument you intend to take. The conclusion should summarise the key points and justify which point was the most important.

To what extent did the importance of councils in the maintenance of political stability decline during the period?

 Spider diagram

Use the information on the opposite page to add detail to the spider diagram below.

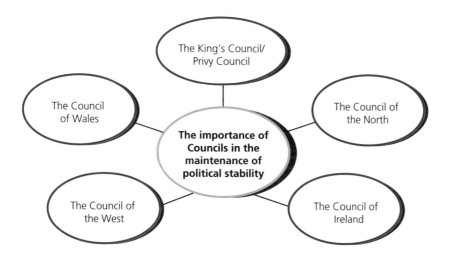

The role of the nobility

Revised

> For a description of all the rebellions mentioned see pages 4–5.

The nobility played a fundamental role in the maintenance of political stability, acting as both the upholders of law and order in the localities, but also having the power and influence to undermine royal authority.

The power of the nobility

- Nobles acted as landowners, with families, such as the Percys and Howards, building up large estates where they ruled their **tenants** like kings. They were able to raise forces from their tenants which threatened the power of the monarch, but the monarch also needed these forces to put down unrest. It was therefore important to the monarch to keep the nobility loyal.
- Nobles acted as local governors, often commanding the following of local gentry, which allowed them to manage local politics. As **Lord Lieutenants** they acted as the Crown's representatives in the counties, commanded the **county militia** and were responsible for justice. As presidents of councils they could influence justice and the raising of troops. They were particularly important in the border areas, which were not visited by monarchs.
- They held influence at court, often as friends of the monarch, but also occupying offices such as **steward** or **chamberlain**. They also had an important role on the Privy Council, although with the emergence of professional advisors such as Thomas **Cromwell** to Henry VIII and William Cecil to Elizabeth I their influence was in decline.
- They had influence in Parliament, either as members of the Lords, or through influencing the election of MPs to the Commons.
- They could become disaffected and challenge the monarch, as was shown by the Earl of Essex in 1601 who objected to the domination of the low-born Cecil family.

Suppression of rebellion

The following table shows the importance of the nobility in the suppression of unrest:

Rebellion	Date	Nobles involved in suppression
Simnel	1486–87	A duke, five earls, a viscount and four barons
Warbeck	1491–97	Earl of Devon, Sir Giles Daubeny and Willoughby de Broke
Amicable Grant	1525	Dukes of Norfolk and Suffolk
Pilgrimage of Grace	1536–37	Earl of Shrewsbury, Duke of Norfolk
Western Rebellion	1549	Lord Russell
Kett's Rebellion	1549	Marquis of Northampton, Earl of Warwick
Wyatt's Rebellion	1554	Duke of Norfolk, Earl of Pembroke
Rebellion of the Northern Earls	1569	Earl of Sussex, Lords Hunsdon, Warwick and Clinton
Irish rebellions	1536–1601	Lords Grey, Mountjoy and Essex

Nobility and the undermining of stability

Despite the importance of nobles in quelling unrest, throughout the period many rebellions were led or supported by nobles (see table, page 28) as they had large households and retainers which could become a private army. When they opposed the regime it could create instability. This was particularly true in Ireland where all rebellions were led by nobles, such as the Earls of Tyrone, Kildare and Desmond.

By the end of the period, the Crown did gradually weaken noble control in vulnerable areas, such as the North. The nobility became less politically ambitious and more respectful of the law.

Complete the paragraph

Below are a sample exam question and a paragraph written in answer to this question. The paragraph contains a point and specific examples, but lacks a concluding explanatory link back to the question. Using the information on the opposite page, on page 70 and from earlier sections of the book, complete the paragraph, adding this link in the space provided.

Assess the importance of the nobility in the maintenance of political stability.

The nobility were important in maintaining stability in the peripheral regions of the country, particularly the North. Some families, such as the Percys, owned large amounts of land and were therefore able to rule as petty kings. They were able to raise considerable forces made up of their tenants, making them indispensable in the maintenance of order. Successive monarchs sought to bring such families under control through acts against livery and maintenance or by appointing local gentry, who owed their office to the Crown, to key jobs. As Lord Lieutenants or as presidents of regional councils the nobility were vital, acting as the principal upholder of order.

_____

_____

Delete as applicable

Below are a sample exam question and a paragraph written in answer to this question. Read the paragraph and decide which of the possible options (in bold) is most appropriate. Delete the least appropriate options and complete the paragraph by justifying your selection.

How far did the importance of the nobility change in the maintenance of stability in the period?

To a **great/fair/limited** extent, the importance of the nobility changed in the maintenance of stability in the period. Henry VII was to a **great/fair/limited** extent reliant upon his nobility for the maintenance of stability. The nobility were **very/not very** important in putting down unrest as was seen by both the Simnel and Cornish Rebellions. This pattern **changed/stayed the same** under Henry VIII when dealing with the Pilgrimage of Grace where nobles such as **Norfolk/Suffolk** were important in negotiating with the rebels. During the reign of Edward and Elizabeth the role of the nobility in putting down disorder **changed/stayed the same** with the use of Russell in 1549 and **Sussex/Essex** in 1569. However, the nobility were also a cause of unrest as seen most noticeably in the reigns of **Henry VII/Henry VIII/Edward VI/Mary Tudor/Elizabeth** when they led rebellions. Overall, to a **great/fair/limited extent**, the importance of the nobility changed in the maintenance of stability in the period because ...

_____

_____

The role of the gentry and the 'middling sort'

For a description of all the rebellions mentioned see pages 4–5.

As the sixteenth century progressed the importance of the gentry and the 'middling sort' in maintaining stability increased. Their inclusion in the running of the Tudor state meant that they no longer provided leadership for rebellions, as had happened with Kett and Wyatt, but instead worked for the state. It can be argued that this change explains why rebellions after 1549 attracted such small numbers and why peasant rebellions, such as Oxfordshire (1596), were poorly led.

The gentry

The most important role of the gentry was as JPs, providing a pivotal link between the Crown and counties. Although JPs had existed in the fourteenth century, their work and numbers increased dramatically in the period 1485–1603. The absence of major rebellions after 1570 may not be solely due to their existence, but they did ensure that the government was better informed and able to respond to local crises, such as the food shortages in the 1590s.

As JPs the gentry had two main roles:

■ **Judicial:** they dispensed justice at a local level, committing to jail those who disturbed the peace and therefore preventing local disturbances from developing into rebellion. They could detain and punish rioters and resolve disputes between masters and servants.

■ **Administrative:** they ensured that statutes were enforced, most importantly controlling the price of grain during food shortages and overseeing the welfare of the poor, both of which were vital in the harsh economic climate of the 1590s.

These roles increased the status of the gentry and, as some also became MPs, moved them up the social ladder. This ensured that they had more in common with the ruling elites than the peasantry, thus encouraging them to remain loyal to the state.

The middling sort

The middling sort were men below the status of gentry, the **yeoman** farmers. Their income was less than the gentry, but they were growing richer. They were often the largest landowners within villages and, as such, seen as the village elites.

In the latter part of the period it was the middling sort who took on roles such as **churchwardens, bailiffs, constables** and **overseers of the poor**, giving them a significant measure of local control. This increased their status within their communities, ensuring that, like the gentry, they had more in common with the higher orders in society. Consequently, the middling sort became increasingly suspicious of the poor and the threat they posed.

The incorporation of the middling sort into the national political culture meant that the Tudor state could count on the support of an increasing number of men who put loyalty to the state above loyalty to their local communities. This was demonstrated in the lack of support for the Oxfordshire Rising in 1596. Those who held local offices had a vested interest in supporting the state and maintaining rather than challenging order.

Support or challenge?

Below is a sample exam question which asks how far you agree with a specific statement. Below this are a series of general statements that are relevant to the question. Using your own knowledge and the information on the opposite page and from the rest of the book, decide whether these statements support or challenge the statement in the question and tick the appropriate box.

'The maintenance of stability owed much to the middling sort.' How far do you agree?

	SUPPORT	CHALLENGE
The dynastic rebellions under Henry VII were defeated by royal and noble forces.		
Local government was firmly in the hands of the nobility at the start of the period.		
The middling sort were active in the Amicable Grant Rising.		
The nobility were important in the maintenance of stability as they led royal forces.		
Many of the Western rebels were from just below the ruling groups.		
Robert Kett was a yeoman.		
Thomas Wyatt was a member of the gentry class.		
The development of institutions such as Parliament increased the role of the gentry in government.		
JPs carried out essential judicial and administrative work that helped to maintain stability.		
The later period saw a reformation in manners.		
The Oxfordshire Rising attracted little support.		
During Elizabeth's reign the middling sort acted as overseers of the poor and churchwardens.		

Simple essay style

Below is a sample exam question. Use your own knowledge, information on the opposite page and information from other sections of the book to produce a plan for this question. Choose four general points, and provide three pieces of specific information to support each general point. Once you have planned your essay, write the introduction and conclusion for the essay. The introduction should list the points to be discussed in the essay and outline the line of argument you intend to take. The conclusion should summarise the key points and justify which point was the most important.

Assess the role of the gentry in maintaining political stability in England and Ireland.

Popular attitudes to authority

For a description of all the rebellions mentioned see pages 4–5.

Tudor monarchs had no standing army or police force to maintain order. Although they developed a series of institutions that helped enforce peace, they also relied on respect. Respect for authority was based on a range of concepts, from the sin of rebelling against a monarch appointed by God, to respect for the head of the household.

The Divine Right of Kings

Although Tudor monarchs did not fully develop the concept of the Divine Right of Kings, they did use the idea that they were appointed by God to help create a sense of mystique and respect. The concept was that God had appointed sovereigns and expected them to be obeyed. Even Henry VII, who had won the throne on the battlefield, claimed he was 'Henry, by the grace of God, King'. However, this idea had less impact when the country was ruled by a Lord Protector or Lord President, such as in the period 1547–53.

The Great Chain of Being

The concept of the **Great Chain of Being** was that everyone was born into a set place in society and that the order was unfaltering. It also taught the themes of loyalty, duty and obligation. However, this applied to those at the top of society as well as the bottom and did not always help in the preservation of peace as the lower orders might look to their superiors for leadership when rebelling, as in the Pilgrimage of Grace (1536–37).

Society of Orders

The Society of Orders also suggested that everyone had their place and role in society. However, this could encourage disquiet if it appeared that the government was showing contempt for the Society of Orders or if gentlemen failed to perform their expected duties. This happened in the rebellions of 1549, when the rebels complained that the gentry were exploiting the economic conditions and not offering help to the lower orders.

The household

The structure of the family helped to uphold the concept of hierarchy and law and order. This was very useful as it was enforced daily. The head of the house was to be obeyed and those who resisted were made to conform. The Church supported this, teaching that obedience to the head of the household was required by God. The family was seen as mirroring the state, with the head of the house the equivalent of the monarch, thus reinforcing the idea of obedience.

A reformation of manners?

The period may also have witnessed a change in attitudes and behaviour, encouraged by the religious developments of the later period. This 'reformation in manners' resulted in people trying to control their behaviour, using litigation rather than unrest to settle disputes and showing a greater willingness to compromise. This development was encouraged by families often praying and reading the Bible together, which helped to reinforce the importance of the household and hierarchy. This had a particular impact on the more wealthy elements of society.

As the gulf between the rich and poor widened over the century the more prosperous discovered that they had less in common with the labourers and peasantry. The wealthy, who owned property, had an interest in upholding order, rather than leading riots. Therefore, by the end of the period, the political nation had grown to include a significant proportion of the population who adopted collective responsibility for the maintenance of law and order.

Turning assertion into argument **a**

Below is a sample question and a series of assertions. Read the exam question and then add a justification to each of the assertions to turn each one into an argument.

How important were changing attitudes to disorder in maintaining stability?

Respect for authority was important to Tudor governments because

_____

_____

Changing attitudes to disorder were also essential in maintaining stability because

_____

_____

Moreover, the gulf between the rich and poor helped maintain stability because

_____

_____

 Recommended reading

Below is a list of suggested further reading on this topic.

- *Access to History: Disorder and Rebellion in Tudor England*, pages 4–8, Nick Fellows (2001)

- *Cambridge Perspectives in History: Authority and Disorder in Tudor Times, 1485–1603*, Paul Thomas (1999)

- *The State and Social Change in Early Modern England 1550–1640*, Chapters 7 and 8, Steve Hindle (2002)

Section 5: Exam focus

The causes of Tudor rebellion

Below is a sample A grade essay. Read the essay and the comments around it.

How far did the causes of rebellion in England remain the same throughout the period 1485–1603?

This is a sound introduction, which sets out a clear line of argument. The candidate is aware of the need to address the issue of the continuity of causes and sets out their thesis. The candidate has provided an overview and a line of argument which will be followed throughout the essay.

Throughout the period 1485–1603 the causes of rebellion under the Tudors centred on four main areas. These were dynastic and factional, taxation and religion. However, by the 'commotion time' of 1549 economic grievances, particularly those regarding enclosures, came to the forefront and were maintained until the end of the period, with the Oxfordshire Rising of 1596.

The opening sentence is crucial as it links straight back to the question. The candidate uses synthesis to show both the continuity and change, which already indicates that the answer is likely to gain high marks.

Throughout the period 1485–1603 dynastic rebellions were present, even though they fluctuated in nature. There were attempts to remove the monarch, as seen in the Simnel and Warbeck Rebellions, which attempted to remove Henry VII, in the Devise of 1553, when Edward VI attempted to exclude Mary and replace her with Lady Jane Grey, and the Northern Earls who wanted to replace Elizabeth with Mary Queen of Scots. This contrasts with attempts to amend the succession in 1536, when the Pilgrim demands attempted to restore Mary Tudor to the line of succession and the Essex Rebellion which wanted to ensure the succession of James VI. Dynastic rebellions were therefore present throughout the period, but were most abundant during the reign of Henry VII who was not secure following his seizure of the throne at the Battle of Bosworth. However, unlike later rebellions these attempted to topple the Tudor regime by securing the throne for Pretenders, such as Perkin Warbeck and Lambert Simnel. However, the attempts made by Thomas Wyatt in 1554 and Westmorland and Northumberland in 1569 put forward legal claimants: Elizabeth and Mary Queen of Scots, respectively. The Earl of Essex's Rebellion in 1601 also conformed to this pattern as he wanted to secure the throne for James VI of Scotland.

Once again the candidate tries to show continuity, although there is some contradiction from the previous paragraph, but this is rectified at the end and the point that dynastic rebellions remained throughout the period has been made.

Dynastic rebellions that attempted to alter the succession remained throughout the period. The demands of the Pilgrims in 1536 sought to restore Mary to the succession after she was ousted by the Act of Succession in 1534. Similarly, the Devise of 1553 attempted to put Lady Jane Grey into the succession and replace Mary Tudor. However, the nature of the claimants meant that the causes were not totally similar, as the Pilgrims attempted to restore Mary, who many believed was the rightful ruler after Edward, whereas the Devise attempted to deprive the rightful ruler.

Taxation rebellions were largely a feature of the early period, particularly the reigns of Henry VII and Henry VIII. However, it cannot be disregarded that Statutes enforced by Somerset in 1549 for taxes on sheep and cloth added to the grievances of the Western Rebels. Similarly, the high taxes resulting from the continued conflict against Spain contributed to the Oxfordshire Rising, suggesting that taxation was a consistent cause, although only subsidiary in the second half of the period. Throughout the reigns of Henry VII and Henry VIII tax rebellions followed the introduction of innovative taxes to finance wars, with Scotland under Henry VII and France in 1525. Both the Cornish and Yorkshire Rebellions were in response to being asked to fund wars in regions that were not usually their responsibility. Tax remained an issue under Henry VIII, but this time protests were against the levels of taxation demanded by the Amicable Grant. Similarly in the Pilgrimage of Grace, the rebels objected to paying because of the high demands, but also the poor harvests. Therefore, as with dynastic unrest, although taxation remained a cause throughout much of the period, the nature of the causes changed and taxation became a subsidiary issue in the latter period.

Factional rebellions were present throughout the period, but again, the nature of the causes did change. During the reign of Henry VII factional unrest resulted in attempts by Yorkists to overthrow the monarch and restore the House of York, through attempts by Lovel and Stafford as well as the use of Pretenders. However, later factional rebellions, although caused by the loss of power and influence, did not attempt to overthrow the monarch, but to restore the influence of the group that had lost favour and attack those who dominated the court. This was seen in the Amicable Grant Rising where Norfolk and Suffolk used it to attack Wolsey and this was repeated in 1536 when the Pilgrims demanded that Cromwell and Lord Rich should be punished, and attempted to restore the influence of the supporters of Catherine of Aragon. However, as the period progressed factionalism became entangled with religion and it can be argued that the 1553 Devise was as much an attempt to preserve Protestantism as it was to secure Northumberland's power. Similarly in 1554 Wyatt's Rebellion could be seen as an attempt to preserve Protestantism by preventing Mary's marriage to Philip of Spain, but was also an attempt to prevent the court from being dominated by Spaniards. Despite this, most factional rebellions were attempts by individuals or groups to reassert their fading power. This was clearly seen with the Aragonese faction in 1536, but also in 1569 with Northumberland and Westmorland, who had lost influence in the North and at court. This was similar with Essex in 1601, as he had lost his political influence with the rise of Robert Cecil.

Economic and social issues were a more significant cause of unrest in the second half of the period. Although the Pilgrims did complain about enclosures and entry fines in 1536, it was only a minor cause of the rising. Economic and social causes became more significant in 1549 when they became a direct cause of both Kett's and the Western Rebellion. Both rebellions complained about enclosures, provoked by Somerset's Enclosure

Once again the opening sentence links back to the question and sets out the line of argument which is developed in the paragraph. There is synthesis as the candidate shows that the causes were similar, reacting to the high levels of taxation. The final sentence links the material back to the question and reinforces the argument.

As with previous paragraphs the opening sentence links directly to the question and the candidate is quick to show both the overall continuity of faction as a cause, but also how it changes. Synthesis is used to compare factional unrest and the supporting detail helps to clinch the point and demonstrate continuity.

The opening sentence establishes the line of argument that is then developed throughout the paragraph. Although there is some supporting detail, this could have been developed. However, the candidate does show that economic causes went from being a subsidiary to a major cause, demonstrating once again the subtlety that is a feature of the response.

The candidate shows clearly that religion was a cause of unrest for only the middle part of the period and demonstrates the continuity by showing how rebellion usually attempted to restore Catholic practices. However, the answer also shows that the pattern is not completely straightforward. The paragraph continues the strong analytical direction that is present throughout the response.

Commission of 1548, and the actions of both sets of rebels, with their attacks on the gentry, such as Hellyons, suggest that class division had also become a cause. Unrest in much of the rest of southern and central England was also concerned with enclosure, suggesting that economic causes had become more important. This would remain until the end of the period, with the Oxfordshire Rising of 1596 the result of enclosure in neighbouring areas. Therefore, although there had been economic causes in the earlier period, they were only underlying causes, but after 1548 they became more significant.

Religion became a cause of rebellion only in 1536 and there were no further religiously motivated rebellions after 1569. It was during this period that religious change caused unrest as both Catholics and Protestants protested against religious innovation and attempted to restore traditional practices. The Pilgrims, Western rebels and Northern Earls all attempted to restore traditional Catholic practices. The Pilgrims complained about the attack on holy days, images and monasteries; the Western rebels complained about the attack on images and chantries; whilst the Northern Earls attempted to restore the Catholic mass. However, perhaps the clearest sign of continuity between these rebellions was the use by all the rebels of the banner of the Five Wounds of Christ. The only exception to this attempt to restore traditional practices was Kett. In this instance the rebels wanted to promote further Protestant practice, hence their demands for improved clerical standards. However, the moderate Elizabethan Settlement helped to end religious unrest so that it was only a feature in the middle of the period.

The candidate reinforces, but also modifies the thesis that was set out in the opening paragraph. This shows that a well thought through essay will not simply use the conclusion to repeat the first paragraph, but will identify nuances and more subtle developments.

During the period 1485–1603 dynastic and factional rebellions were ever present, but the former declined in severity, whereas factional unrest remained. However, there were also changes to the causes of unrest. Taxation declined as a cause of rebellion, from a major cause under Henry VII and the early years of Henry VIII, to a subsidiary cause in the mid-Tudor period. Economic and religious causes only emerged in the middle and later period, but economic causes would remain through the rest of the century, whereas religious rebellions disappeared after 1569. However, as most rebellions were multi causal, there were elements of economic and social grievances in some of the earlier rebellions, suggesting that the major causes of rebellion were present, with the exception of religion, throughout the period, but what changed was their relative importance.

50/60

The essay contains relevant and accurate knowledge, which is used to drive the argument forward. It is clearly structured and the argument is coherent and easy to follow. The answer focuses on change and continuity over time and relates the material back to the actual question. The answer is mostly focused, although there are some slightly weaker sections.

Moving to the very top of the highest level

Using the comments and the mark scheme on page 3, make a list of additional features that would enable this answer to achieve full marks. Remember that an answer receiving full marks is not a perfect answer, but one that is 'best fit' with the level descriptors in the mark scheme.

Below is a sample A grade essay. Read the essay and the comments around it.

To what extent did Tudor rebellions in England fail to achieve any of their aims?

The opening paragraph offers a clear view of the line of argument the candidate intends to pursue, although there are some variations to this pattern. The thesis offered is straightforward and clear and a reading of the final paragraph will show whether this has been followed through the whole essay.

Throughout the period 1485–1603 Tudor rebellions largely failed to achieve any of their aims whether dynastic, economic or religious. However, the success in bringing about the abandonment of the Amicable Grant in 1525 and the piecemeal successes made by the Lincolnshire rebels and the Pilgrims in 1536 in slowing down the abandonment of some Catholic practices shows that not all Tudor rebellions failed to achieve their aims; but in the main rebellion still ended in defeat.

The opening sentence is linked back to the actual question; the qualification shows that the candidate has thought about the issues. There is some evidence of continuity and synthesis, shown through the final section on the defeat of dynastic unrest during the reign of Henry VII.

Dynastic rebellions throughout the period failed in the main to achieve their aims. However, the success of Henry VII at Bosworth in 1485 and the limited success of Lady Jane Grey through Northumberland's coup of 1553 show that not all Tudor rebellions were complete failures. The Yorkist monarchy was successfully toppled in 1485 and the succession of Mary was successfully challenged in 1553, albeit for only nine days. However, the main dynastic rebellions such as Lovel and Stafford in 1486, Simnel in 1486–87 and Warbeck in 1491–97, failed to achieve any of their aims. Simnel's defeat was because of the royal army at Stoke, but in the 1490s, when Warbeck was successfully driven from Ireland and England, it was the lack of support from either foreign mercenaries or nobility, which condemned the rising to failure.

The opening sentence offers a view about the theme to be discussed. There is some evidence of synthesis. The argument is balanced, although the candidate does suggest that some of the economic gains were not the direct result of rebellion as they were much later.

Economic rebellions throughout the period 1536–96 achieved some limited successes in fulfilling their aims. The Western rebels of 1549 successfully managed to prevent the levying of the unpopular Sheep and Cloth tax. However, neither the Western nor Kett's rebels were able to end enclosure or the loss of common land. Similarly, in 1596, the Oxfordshire rebels were unable to halt the progress of enclosure. Despite this, the demands of the Pilgrims in 1536 and Kett's rebels to reduce entry fines and improve wages were partially met, although the issue of wages was only resolved in 1563 with the Statute of Artificers, which fixed maximum not minimum wages, hardly a direct result of the unrest. However, in most instances the lack of cross-class support for low politics and economic rebellions meant that they largely failed to achieve their aims and at best made piecemeal gains.

Taxation rebellions were the most successful of all Tudor rebellions, with most achieving at least some success and making some limited gains throughout the period 1489–1549. The Yorkshire and Cornish Rebellions of 1489 and 1497 both achieved their aims as they successfully stopped the taxes designed to fund wars in France and Scotland respectively. However, despite this success the Cornish rebels suffered a crushing military defeat at Blackheath and this was coupled with economic sanctions that were imposed on the area after their defeat. The Amicable Grant Rising of 1525, unlike either 1489 or 1497, was a complete success. As well as the tax not being collected, which was the main aim of the rebels, the aftermath of the rebellion, unlike 1497, resulted in no slaughter of the rebels, just the abandonment of the tax. Similar success can be seen with the Sheep tax of 1549, which, like the Amicable Grant in 1525, the rebels were able to stop.

Factional rebellions were present throughout the period but had very limited success. Both the Amicable Grant and the Pilgrimage of Grace which hoped to remove the king's ministers, Wolsey and Cromwell, may have succeeded in planting seeds of discontent in Henry's mind as both Wolsey and Cromwell fell four years later, but did not achieve immediate success and their falls cannot be directly linked to the unrest. Both the Northern Earls' and Essex's Rebellion, which aimed to remove the Cecil faction, failed as the family dominated politics throughout Elizabeth's reign. Perhaps the overthrow of Somerset by Northumberland can be seen as the only successful factional incident as throughout the period those in favour were able to maintain the support of the monarch and therefore defeat their challengers.

Religious rebellions in the period 1536–69 had little success in achieving their aims. Religious rebellions attempted to reverse the religious changes that the government had implemented. The Pilgrimage of Grace may have speeded up the process of dissolution, encouraging full suppression in 1539. However, the rebellion might also have encouraged Henry to adopt a more conservative approach, with the Six Articles, but this gain was insignificant when compared with their demands to restore Catholicism to the position of pre 1529. Compared to this limited success, the Western rebels and Northern Earls achieved even less. The Western rebels' protest against the moderate Prayer Book led to an even more Protestant Second Prayer Book in 1552, whilst the Northern Earls saw no restoration of Catholic practices and instead the full implementation of the Elizabethan Religious Settlement and the increased Protestantisation of the North.

The response is very clear that taxation rebellions were the most successful of all rebellions. The response supports the claim with precise details and shows synthesis. The paragraph is consistently analytical and the candidate does support their claim, although no comparison is made with other rebellions to establish the point that taxation rebellions were the most successful and this will limit the final mark.

A theme is established and a clear line of argument is pursued. The answer shows continuity of failure to remove ministers and reassert the importance of a rival group across the period. There is synthesis across the period, although a concluding sentence pulling the paragraph together would have been beneficial and helped to take the essay into the higher levels.

The conclusion does slightly modify the opening paragraph, but the answer does not deviate significantly from the original thesis. The candidate does make a valid point, that when some aims were achieved they were often the subsidiary aims and this could have been developed in the main body of the essay.

Overall, throughout the Tudor period not all rebellions failed to achieve any of their aims, however only the Amicable Grant Rising was completely successful. Some rebellions did achieve some of their subsidiary aims, such as the Western Rebellion over the Sheep Tax, or were successful in the short term, as with Lady Jane Grey. Some economic grievances were addressed, as in 1536 and 1549, but both sets of rebels failed to achieve their main aims of reversing religious changes. Even with economic rebellions, the main concerns were not really addressed until the 1590s, when, faced with serious food shortages, Elizabeth's government introduced a range of measures to ameliorate the situation. Religious rebellions failed to prevent the implementation of government policy. As a result, it was only taxation rebellions, notably those of 1489, 1497 and 1525, which achieved their main aims, suggesting that although most failed to achieve their aims, not all did.

46/60

Although the essay shows a good understanding of continuity and change across the period and supports the arguments with relevant and accurate material, some paragraphs lack the developed judgements needed for the highest levels. There is good explanation and analysis of the topic, but in places it is uneven, as in the paragraphs on taxation and faction. The answer does remain focused on the question set and there is evidence of synthesis throughout.

Reverse engineering

The best essays are based on careful plans. Read the essay and the comments and try to work out the general points of the plan used to write the essay. Once you have done this, note down the specific examples used to support each general point and, where examples are either weak or lacking, use this book to help you find precise details.

The impact of disturbances on Tudor governments

Revised

Below is a sample A grade essay. Read the essay and the comments around it.

How effectively did Tudor governments deal with unrest?

The opening sentence sets out a clear line of argument and this is briefly developed to show that the governments were more effective in England than Ireland. There is clear focus on the question and the answer also establishes some criteria against which the concept of 'how effectively' will be judged.

During the course of the period 1485–1603 there was a decline in the severity of the threat from rebellions and also a decline in their frequency, suggesting that as the period progressed governments became more adept and effective at dealing with unrest, particularly in England. Henry VII faced rebellions throughout his whole reign, with Warbeck's lasting for much of the 1490s, whereas Essex's Rebellion in 1601 was defeated within a few hours. This view is given further credence by the declining numbers who took part in rebellion, with Essex able to raise only a few hundred and the Oxfordshire Rising of 1596 just four, whereas earlier rebellions such as the Pilgrimage of Grace attracted 40,000. Most persuasively, the poor economic conditions of the 1590s, the worst of the century, failed to stimulate unrest, suggesting that the government's legislation had been particularly effective in diminishing the causes of unrest. However, governments were less effective in dealing with Irish rebellions, which often lasted for years, with Tyrone's lasting from 1595 to 1603.

The candidate develops the theme of winning support for the regime, largely focusing on the nobility. There is evidence of the change in effectiveness across the period. The answer reinforces the point about the nobility's importance by a clever comparison of developments in 1549, showing a very clear understanding of the importance of the nobility.

Without a standing army or a police force to maintain order, the government relied on the support of the nobility and gentry to put down unrest in the localities. Not only had the government become more effective in winning noble support, but as the century progressed they were also able to win over the 'middling sort'. This left the peasants as the only significant group who would rebel but deprived them of leadership. At the start of the period, Henry VII faced numerous rebellions which involved the nobility and he was unsure of support, as shown by Stanley's involvement in the Warbeck conspiracy. However, through rewards and patronage the government was able to build up support so that in 1569 when the Northern Earls rebelled the Council of the North was able to put down the unrest with relative ease. Similarly, Elizabeth was able to count on the support of nobles and the city of London to quickly defeat Essex. Government reliance on the nobility was also effective in 1549. It was only in the two areas of East Anglia and the West Country where there were power vacuums, due to the absence of nobles, that unrest developed into rebellion. However, in areas such as Sussex, Arundel was able to disperse rioters, suggesting that as the period progressed the reliance upon the nobility was largely effective.

The candidate takes a synoptic approach, showing that military action was not an effective way of dealing with unrest across the whole period. There is a good range of examples and the answer makes comparisons between England and Ireland, which is an important aspect of the question.

However, the government was not always effective in dealing with rebels. This was particularly true at the start of the period when Henry VII was twice forced into battle by rebels at Stoke and Blackheath. Although the king was victorious, battles were risky. Henry himself had seized the throne by force and the result of Stoke could easily have been reversed, particularly as the support of some nobles was not guaranteed. Similarly, in 1549 government forces under Northampton were defeated at Norwich and it took Russell five attempts to finally crush the

Western rebels. Military force was also ineffective in Ireland as the rebels often avoided full-scale military confrontation, instead retreating into the mountains or wastelands. Even when the Irish were defeated, as in 1583, Tyrone was still able to raise an even larger force which defeated the English, and it was not until Mountjoy's arrival that the government was finally able to crush it.

Military action was not only risky, but also costly and it took the monarch time to gather together a large enough force to deal with large-scale risings. As a consequence, the government often resorted to negotiations with rebels. The effectiveness of this policy varied. The government was able to persuade the rebels involved in protests against the Amicable Grant to disperse and similarly Norfolk was able to negotiate with the Pilgrims, despite being outnumbered by the rebel forces five to one. However, negotiation was not always successful. Neither Kett's rebels or the Western rebels were willing to disperse as a result of either pardons or negotiations. This forced the government to abandon its garrisoning policy in Scotland and commit large numbers of troops at the very time the country was under threat of invasion from France. Similarly, in Ireland, negotiations between O'Neill and the English commanders in both 1596 and 1599 failed to end the unrest.

Government strategy in dealing with rebellions became more effective as the period progressed. At the start, government policy had been largely reactive, particularly during the reign of Henry VII. He sent troops to deal with threats and challenges, such as Simnel, the Yorkshire Rebellion, Cornish Rebellion and Warbeck. However, as the period progressed the policy changed and the government became more effective as it took action through parliamentary legislation to prevent unrest from breaking out. This was particularly true in the period after 1549. The effectiveness of government legislation in dealing with social and economic issues was most apparent in the 1590s when, despite a run of poor harvests and high grain prices, unrest was limited to the Oxfordshire Rising. The issuing of Books of Orders to JPs and legislation on the movement of grain, along with the introduction of Poor Laws, all helped to dispel disquiet.

The greatest threat to Tudor rule came from dynastic challenges and the government was largely effective in removing this threat in England, but threats to their power in Ireland were more difficult to eradicate. Henry VII was ultimately able to remove the Yorkist challenge, not only by executing the Pretenders but with the death of the Earl of Lincoln, arrest of Suffolk and execution of Stafford. Similarly, the Courtenays were removed by Henry VIII, Mary Tudor destroyed the Greys following Lady Jane Grey's defeat and Elizabeth was able to arrest and execute Mary Queen of Scots. However, in Ireland the situation was more difficult as Tyrone was able to raise a nationwide revolt against Elizabeth that lasted over eight years. Despite these challenges, a regime that had seized the throne on the battlefield, with a limited claim to the throne, was able to maintain the throne for over 100 years.

The paragraph discusses negotiation and its effectiveness, but would have benefited from a judgement as to the overall effectiveness of this as a method for managing unrest. However, there is evidence of synthesis and again there is an attempt to make a comparison with developments in Ireland.

The opening sentence sets out a clear line of argument and the answer shows how the government response became more effective as the period progressed. Although there is a synoptic approach, the paragraph would benefit from some more precise support. There might also be some comparison with Ireland.

The paragraph adopts a thematic approach, considering how effective governments were in dealing with the dynastic threat. The answer displays a good level of synthesis across the period and a comparison is made with Ireland. Most significantly, the answer also reaches a clear judgement.

The answer maintains its thematic approach and has a clear line of argument, comparing the treatment of rebels in Ireland with England. The paragraph is always analytical and shows both change and continuity across the period, with well-chosen examples to support the claims.

The government's treatment of rebels was usually effective in England, but its handling of Irish unrest suggested that it had little sympathy for or understanding of the grievances there. In Ireland, the government seized lands, imposed fines and destroyed property. This did not deter future unrest and may have provoked further hatred which leaders such as Desmond and Tyrone were able to exploit. However, in England the government was more effective. Weaker monarchs such as Henry VII and Mary were more lenient in their treatment of rebels as they were unsure of support, whereas Henry VIII and Elizabeth were harsher. Henry VII, through forgiving those who subsequently showed loyalty to the regime, was able to win support, but only after he had exacted heavy fines, whereas Henry VIII was vindictive in his treatment of the Pilgrims and went back on his promise of pardon after Bigod's Rising. However, this approach was largely effective as the northern counties were relatively quiet in 1549 and very few rose in support of the Northern Earls in 1569, suggesting they had not forgotten the previous punishments. Similarly, the numbers put to death by Edward VI's regime after 1549 was effective in discouraging later peasant unrest and may explain why so few joined Wyatt or rebelled under Elizabeth. When there was unrest under Elizabeth, as in Oxfordshire, the response was draconian as a warning to other potential rebels, and appears to have been effective as the country remained quiet despite the poor economic conditions.

The response reaches a valid conclusion, based on the argument that has been put forward in each paragraph. The answer has maintained its focus on 'how effectively' and not drifted into a discussion of success. Even in the conclusion there is evidence of synthesis with a comparison of the duration of unrest.

Most rebellions were localised affairs, protesting against policies and ministers. Although lengthy rebellions were an irritant and could undermine credibility in the government, as with Somerset in 1549, most English disturbances were over quickly suggesting the government was effective in dealing with them, with only the Pilgrimage, Western and Kett lasting more than a month. The strategies of propaganda, persuasion and threats usually maintained the support of the nobility and clergy and, by the end of the period, the gentry and middling sort. The policy of 'buying time' was usually effective and was less dangerous or costly than military confrontation. However, once the government was in a strong position, the use of reprisals against leaders was often effective in discouraging further unrest. It was only in Ireland that the government was less effective because the absence of permanent garrisons, the terrain and the increased unpopularity of government policies meant that it was difficult to maintain order, and this difficulty only increased as the period progressed.

52/60

The answer remains focused on the question of 'how effectively' throughout and in most paragraphs reaches a valid judgement about the theme under discussion. The analysis is usually fully developed and the argument is well supported by appropriate and relevant examples. The answer also considers the question in terms of Ireland, an issue that is often ignored by candidates.

Reaching judgements

In order to reach the very top level candidates need to reach judgements about the theme they are considering in relation to the question. Identify the paragraphs where the candidate has successfully done this and those where a judgement is either absent or is not developed. In the latter cases write a couple of sentences for each of the paragraphs so that a judgement based on the argument is reached.

The maintenance of political stability

Below is a sample A grade essay. Read the essay and the comments around it.

How far did England become more politically stable during the period from 1485 to 1603?

The answer introduces a clear line of argument and a series of themes that can be built on in the rest of the essay. The answer also hints at a balanced discussion, rather than a one-sided argument, which could not reach the higher levels.

At the start of the period, Henry Tudor seized the throne on the battlefield, yet in 1603 on the death of Elizabeth, the throne was passed on peacefully, despite Elizabeth's lack of a child, suggesting that at least the succession was more stable. Similarly, the decline in the frequency and severity of unrest in the period after 1549 also supports the view that England was more stable. Riot and rebellion were no longer the method used by most to resolve differences; instead Parliament or litigation was more popular. However, despite these developments there was still some evidence of instability as factional disputes continued throughout the period.

The answer adopts a synoptic approach through a comparison between the start and the end of the period. There is evidence of very strong synthesis in the paragraph, suggesting that if this is maintained it will reach a very high level. There are very precise factual details to support the points.

The decline in the frequency and severity of rebellion suggests that England was more politically stable by 1603. Rebellion had been a fairly constant feature of Henry VII's reign, with him forced into battle at Stoke against Simnel to defend his throne. However, under Elizabeth there were only three rebellions, with the Northern Earls the most serious, attracting 5000 supporters. When this is compared to rebellions earlier in the period, such as the Pilgrimage of Grace in 1536 which attracted 40,000 rebels, it is clear that the appeal of rebellion had declined. Moreover, the other two rebellions towards the end of Elizabeth's reign attracted even less support, with the Oxfordshire Rising attracting only four and the Essex Rebellion being defeated in under twelve hours, whereas both the Western Rebellion and Kett's in 1549 had lasted over a month. However, despite these developments, it should be remembered that Essex had still been able to raise a rebellion in Elizabeth's capital city, suggesting that stability was not completely assured.

The focus is on change and continuity, showing that England was less stable at the start of the period because of the dynastic challenges, but became more stable as rebellions no longer aimed to overthrow the established political system. The answer is balanced and reaches an overall judgement based on the analysis.

Earlier rebellions had also presented a far greater threat to the stability of the nation as many were politically motivated and aimed at the overthrow of the monarch, with Lovel, Stafford, Simnel and Warbeck all aiming to replace Henry VII with a Yorkist claimant. These political challenges to the Tudors would continue until 1553 with Northumberland's attempted coup to replace Mary Tudor with Lady Jane Grey. However, political stability increased as low politics replaced high politics as a cause of unrest. Politically motivated rebellions gave way to economically driven unrest, which was less threatening as it lacked support from the nobility or gentry and therefore was usually poorly led, as with the Oxfordshire Rising. But, despite this development, factional disputes continued throughout the period. This continuity was evident with attempts in 1536 by the Aragonese faction to regain influence, in 1553 as Northumberland tried to maintain power, in 1554 when Wyatt attempted to limit Spanish influence and in the Essex Rebellion in 1601, resulting from the domination of the Cecils. However, despite these struggles, the regime was not destabilised, as even in 1549 the transition of power to Northumberland as Lord President of the Council was smooth, suggesting that even at potential crisis points stability was far greater than in 1485 when Henry had to fight for his throne.

Stability was also increased by the decline in religious conflict which had been a feature of the mid-Tudor period. At the start of the period religion had been a bond holding society together, but the changes brought about after the break with Rome created instability, with the Pilgrimage of Grace, the Western Rebellion and the Northern Earls seeking to preserve their traditional religious practices and institutions. However, the moderate Elizabethan Religious Settlement lessened tension, reflected in the lack of support for the papal bull of 1570, which excommunicated Elizabeth, or the Armada in 1588. The Elizabethan broad-based Church did much to reduce religious tension, which had the potential to be a cause of instability.

The nature and role of the nobility changed during the period and this helped bring about increased political stability. Instead of a nobility whose instinct was fighting, as had been apparent during the reigns of Henry VII and Henry VIII, Elizabeth's nobles were more willing to serve the state, were loyal and saw the monarch as the source of rewards and patronage. Under the early Tudors, the nobility had the ability to raise large forces of retainers and directly challenge the monarch, but under Elizabeth, noble unrest was usually the last resort of the desperate, as with Northumberland, Westmorland and Essex, all of whom felt so excluded from power that they had nothing to lose. However, nobles were more likely to be found on the side of the monarch. They supplied troops to crush unrest, as with Hunsdon and Sussex in 1569, acted as Lord Lieutenants to prevent the outbreak of rebellion, or negotiated with rebels as with Arundel in 1549. Many nobles had increased their wealth through patronage and rewards and therefore had too much to lose in rebelling. Instead, they used the law courts or Parliament to resolve disputes. Their unwillingness to be involved in unrest also helped deprive potential rebels of leadership and further limit the likelihood of unrest.

Similarly, both the gentry and the 'middling sort' had, by the end of the period, allied themselves with the Crown and were unwilling to lead rebellions, unlike in 1549 or 1554 with Kett and Wyatt. As a consequence, the Crown had the support and backing of the political nation. The growing use of Parliament as a sounding board for policy involved many in decision-making and membership of Parliament became a status symbol that they were unwilling to risk losing through revolting. However, the increased use of Parliament did, to some extent, mean that disputes were transferred there. Those just below gentry status also gained from the rewards of office-holding. The middling sort became churchwardens, Poor Law Commissioners

The answer is well structured with the focus on change and continuity; comparisons across the period are made. The argument is well supported with precise and relevant evidence.

The answer maintains its thematic approach and once again compares the start and end of the period to support the overall argument. The argument is supported by precise examples and the last sentence links back to the question.

This paragraph builds on the previous one and shows a clear structure to the response. The increase in political stability was, at least in part, the result of winning over the support of other sections of society. There are precise examples to back up the claim.

and Parish Constables, raising their status within their communities and distancing themselves from the lower orders. The incorporation of such groups in the state and their realisation that their interests were better served by supporting the state significantly reduced the potential for unrest, depriving the lower orders of leadership.

Even among the lower orders there was less inclination to rebel. Even during the 1590s, when there was a series of poor harvests, legislation was successful in improving conditions and discouraging unrest. Statutes limited the export of grain and the Books of Orders for JPs controlled supplies, helping to maintain stability. Moreover, it appeared as if the lower orders had realised that rebellion usually ended in failure and often death. The memories of 1549 at both Dussindale and Clyst Heath were a reminder that rebellion was not an effective way to resolve disputes. Their lives were already nasty, brutish and short and there was no need to add to this by rioting, which may explain why only four men turned up for the 1596 Oxfordshire Rising.

The growth and development of governing institutions and bodies throughout the period, such as the Privy Council, councils in the regions and Parliament, and the development of offices, such as Lord Lieutenant, all helped to increase government control and ensure that laws were enforced and upheld. The Tudor monarchy became more stable the longer it ruled, as shown in its ability to survive the weak rule of Edward VI and Mary Tudor. There were disputes, even in the last years of Elizabeth's reign, and the threat of invasion from the war with Spain, but the monarch had the support of more of the nation than had been the case in 1485, making England much more stable than it had been.

The theme of winning the support of a range of social groups is continued. The paragraph would benefit from a more overt link back to the issue of stability, rather than leaving it implied.

The conclusion reflects the line of argument pursued throughout the essay and although the institutional developments mentioned in this paragraph could have been developed as a separate issue, the answer has covered a wide range of issues and themes and it would be unrealistic to expect everything to be covered in the time allowed.

54/60

A very strong answer, although there are some slightly weaker areas, as in the section on religion or the penultimate paragraph, which prevent it from reaching the very top. However, it is well organised and easy to follow, with a balanced discussion leading to a well-supported conclusion.

What makes a good synoptic answer?

You have now considered four sample A grade essays. Use these essays to make a bullet-pointed list of the characteristics of an A grade synoptic essay. Use this list when planning and writing your own practice exam essays.

Glossary

Act of Six Articles An act that upheld traditional Catholic practices and remained in force until 1547

Acts of Attainder Acts passed by Parliament against traitors which took away the traitor's land and their family's land

Arable Used or suitable for growing crops such as corn or wheat

Aragonese Supporters of Henry VIII's queen, Catherine of Aragon. After the divorce and her death a group of her followers put pressure on Henry to ensure her daughter, Mary Tudor, was restored to the succession

Armada The naval invasion force sent by Philip II of Spain to invade England in 1588

Articles A list of grievances drawn up by rebels

Bailiff The agent of a landlord, responsible for the running of an estate

Bigod's Rising This rising in 1537 was the final part of the Pilgrimage of Grace. The numbers who rose, believing Henry would not keep his promises, were much smaller than in 1536, which allowed Henry to crush the rising and ignore his earlier promises

Bonds and recognisances Bonds bound people to the Crown to undertake a certain action or pay money. A recognisance was the acknowledgement to fulfil the commitment

Castleward A former military service which required tenants to defend Norwich Castle. It was replaced by the payment of rent

Catholic recusants Catholics who did not attend their local parish churches. At the start of the Elizabethan period many had attended, but with the influence of missionary priests many were encouraged to stay away

Cecil faction The supporters of William, and later Robert, Cecil

Chamberlain The manager of the monarch's household

Chantries Chapels where prayers for the dead were said to reduce their time in purgatory

Churchwardens Officers responsible for the financial arrangements of their parish churches

Common land Grazing land in a village that was available for everyone, even if they owned no land. It was not fenced

Constables The governors of a royal castle

Council of the North Established by Richard III to run the area north of the Trent, the Council was based in York. It was reformed after both the Pilgrimage of Grace and the rebellion of the Northern Earls

County levy A local body of troops raised in a county

County militia The part-time armed force raised by each county, organised by the Lord Lieutenant

Coup The illegal seizure of power, usually by force

Cranmer Thomas Cranmer defended Henry VIII's divorce from Catherine of Aragon and was appointed Archbishop of Canterbury in 1533. He wrote the Prayer Book during Edward VI's reign, but was burned for his beliefs by Mary

Cromwell Thomas Cromwell was Henry VIII's chief minister after the fall of Thomas Wolsey and until his own fall and execution in 1540

Debased the coinage Reduced the gold and silver content of the coinage, whilst keeping the value of the coins the same. This helped to cause inflation as people did not trust the new coinage and so prices rose

Decaying towns In the sixteenth century many towns were in economic decline and suffered from the problems of high unemployment and poverty

Deputy Lieutenant Assisted Lord Lieutenants in the running of the county. They usually came from the leading gentry

Devise The document by which Edward VI attempted to deprive Mary of the throne and replace her with Lady Jane Grey

Duke of Somerset The Lord Protector of Edward VI who ruled England from Henry VIII's death in 1547 until his fall following the rebellions of 1549. He was restored to the Council, but was executed in 1552

Elizabethan Religious Settlement This usually refers to the Acts of Uniformity and Supremacy passed at the start of Elizabeth I's reign, which established a moderate form of Protestantism. It established the organisation, ritual and teaching of the Church

Enclosure The hedging of land, often with common grazing rights, by a landlord in order to graze large flocks of sheep

Enclosure Commission Established by Lord Protector Somerset in 1548 to look into enclosures and determine their legality

English Bibles A number of Bibles were produced in English, but the first official version was the Great Bible in 1540; this replaced the Latin Bible and made the Bible more available to those who could read

Entry fine A fee paid by tenants to renew their lease or by a new tenant following the death of the previous tenant

Excommunication The formal exclusion of a person from the Church, condemning that person to eternal damnation

Exeter Conspiracy In 1538 the government claimed to have uncovered a plot. The plot was named after the Marquis of Exeter, Henry Courtenay, who was supposed to have conspired with his brothers to overthrow Henry VIII and restore Catholicism. It resulted in the execution of the Marquis, Lord Montague and the elderly Countess of Salisbury

Faction A group of people with similar views who joined together in order to gain influence and remove those who were influencing the monarch

Five Wounds of Christ A banner that displayed the five wounds of Christ following his crucifixion

Fixed rate An agreed rate that could not be changed

Folding cattle Allowing cattle and sheep to graze on land after the harvest in order to manure it

Food riots Shortages of grain in the 1580s and 1590s which resulted in food riots in the south of England, notably Somerset, Kent, Sussex, Gloucestershire and Hampshire

Forced loans A tax raised without the approval of Parliament

Francis I King of France from 1515 to 1547. His main rival was the Holy Roman Emperor, but Henry VIII also saw him as a rival and England was in frequent conflict with France, often in alliance with the Emperor

Garrison The placing of soldiers in a town to protect it

Gentry The class below the nobility. They were usually men of some wealth and land holding from well-bred families

Grants of monopolies Under Elizabeth I rights were given to courtiers to be the sole manufacturer or trader in a certain article. This allowed them to set their own prices

Great Council Meetings of the nobles of the kingdom, called to give the monarch advice. Used frequently by Henry VII

Guerrilla warfare Irregular fighting, usually avoiding open warfare and conducted by smaller forces against larger ones

Heretics People who departed from the established beliefs of the Catholic Church; the usual punishment was burning

High politics Politics surrounding issues such as the succession that affected the ruling classes rather than low politics, which surrounded issues such as enclosure that affected the lower classes

Holy Roman Emperor The elected ruler of lands that today include Germany. The authority of the Holy Roman Emperor was limited (more in theory than in reality) and much of the area was ruled by independent princes

Homilies Official lessons that priests could read to the congregation

Hosts The various regional armies that were formed in the north of England during the Pilgrimage of Grace

Household servants The personal servants and staff of the monarch or noble. The monarch's household servants were part of the Court

Inflation A rise in prices relative to wages so that the purchasing power of wages declines

Injunctions A series of orders issued by Cromwell to priests. It instructed them about what should be taught and how churches should be decorated

Innovative taxation New forms of taxation or taxation that ignored traditional practices

Jesuits Members of the religious order founded by Ignatius Loyola in 1540; known for their strict discipline and loyalty

JP Justice of the Peace. Appointed for every county, they served for a year. They were unpaid and usually local gentry whose job it was to see that laws were obeyed in the county. They gradually replaced sheriffs and during the Tudor period they took on an increasing number of responsibilities

Jurisdictional control The power to make legal decisions over certain areas

Lord Deputy Appointed by the monarch to rule Ireland in the name of the monarch

Lord Lieutenant Appointed by the monarch; one for each county. Their main task was to organise the county militia

Lord President of the Council The title taken by the Duke of Northumberland when he replaced the Duke of Somerset as head of the Regency Council

Lord Protector The title given to the Duke of Somerset when he headed the Regency Council to rule during the minority of Edward VI

Magistrate An official who runs a legal court that deals with minor offences

Martial law The replacement of civil rule by military rule

Mercenaries Overseas professional soldiers who were paid to fight

Minor The term used to describe a child before he or she attains majority (the age of full legal responsibility) and is able to act independently

Missionary priests A priest from overseas sent to help with the conversion of a country

Non-parliamentary tax A levy without parliment's permission

Oaths of Succession and Supremacy Oaths given to office holders following Henry VIII's divorce, which involved swearing to accept the change in the succession and his right to be Head of the Church

Overseers of the poor Officials whose job it was to administer the Poor Law and distribute relief

Pale The area around Dublin where English rule was secure

Papacy The authority or office of the Pope

Papal bull A decree issued by the Pope

Papal sanction The approval of the Pope

Particularism Allegiance to the local area before the country. This declined as the sixteenth century progressed

Pasture Land used for the grazing of sheep

Peasants' Revolt In 1381 Kent and Essex, under John Ball and Watt Tyler, revolted against new and high levels of taxation to fund war against France

Peerages The granting of noble status

Penal laws Laws passed in the 1570s that punished non-attendance at church

Peripheral The regions on the edge of England, such as the borders with Scotland or the West Country

Pilgrims' ballad A song written by the protestors during the Pilgrimage of Grace; it criticised many of the King's ministers

Plantation system A system in Ireland which involved land being taken from rebels and granted to English and local landlords at reduced rates

Poor Laws Laws brought in during the sixteenth century to look after the poor following the closure of the monasteries. The laws gradually discriminated between different types of poor, punishing those who could work but did not do so, and giving aid to those who were unable to work due to illness or their age

Prayer Book The book containing the order of services to be used in church. This was changed during the reign of Edward VI and the new Prayer Book issued in 1549 provoked the Western Rebellion

Pretenders People who make a false claim to a title or the throne. For example, the Yorkists put forward Simnel and Warbeck who claimed to be the Earl of Warwick and the Duke of York respectively. They had stronger claims to the throne than Henry VII

Princes in the Tower The children of Edward IV who were arrested and supposedly murdered by Richard III to remove challenges to his takeover of power

Privy Council A body of advisors, chosen by the monarch. It was their duty to carry out royal commands

Prorogue To end a parliamentary session without dissolving Parliament. This meant that the Parliament could be recalled

Provincialism Loyalty to the local area or county rather than the country

Reformation The religious changes that saw England break away from the Catholic Church and establish a separate, independent Church of which the monarch was the head

Relics Religious artefacts, claimed to be the remains or personal belongings of a saint or other religious figure

Richard II He was overthrown as king of England in 1399 by Henry Bolingbroke. The performance of the play *Richard II* reminded people that the removal of a monarch had a precedent

Royal progresses Official journeys made by the monarch around the country, usually in the summer months and confined to southern and central England. During the journey, the monarch would stay with nobles and members of the gentry

Serfs Peasants who are tied to the land on which they work

Sheep and Cloth tax Taxes on the size of sheep flocks and the production of cloth that Edward VI's government proposed introducing in 1549

Sheep-corn areas Areas of mixed farming where grain was grown and sheep were raised

Sheriff The chief officer of the Crown in each county

Silken Thomas A member of the Kildare clan, who were seen as the natural rulers of the Pale

Standing army A full-time army. England did not have the finances to pay for one

Star Chamber The members of the Royal Council who dealt with legal matters

Statute of Uses A law which altered the way property could be left in a will

Steward An officer of the royal household, often responsible for running Crown lands

Stone altars Traditional altars in Catholic churches were made of stone, but during Edward's reign they were replaced with wooden altars. This was symbolic of the change in the meaning of the Eucharist from a sacrifice to an act of remembrance

Subsidy A parliamentary tax

Subsidy Act An Act of Parliament agreeing to the levying of a certain amount of money

Sweat, the A form of influenza

Tenants Farmers who did not own the land they farmed, but rented it for a fixed rent for a certain number of years

Treaty of Ayton Treaty signed by Henry VII with Scotland in 1497, in which Scotland ended their support for Warbeck

Treaty of Etaples Treaty signed by Henry VII with France in 1492, in which the French agreed not to give support to Yorkist Pretenders and to pay a pension to the English king

Ulster A province in the north of Ireland

Usurper A person who seizes power illegally

Visitations Inspections that involved questioning either monks or clergy about the conditions in monasteries and churches

Wage labourers Workers who rely solely on wages for their income

Warrant A document allowing the arrest, search or seizure of goods

Wolsey Cardinal Thomas Wolsey became a royal councillor in 1510, but rose to prominence through organising the expedition against France in 1513. He became Henry's chief minister and was also made a cardinal. He began to lose Henry's trust following the failure of the Amicable Grant, and more significantly when he could not obtain Henry's divorce from Catherine of Aragon

Writ A legal command ordering a person to act or behave in a certain way

Yeomen Farmers below the rank of gentry, but who owned their own land and made a substantial income from it

Yorkists Supporters of the House of York, who had fought in the Wars of the Roses in the fifteenth century against the House of Lancaster. The family had a strong claim to the throne through relatives of the previous monarchs Edward IV and Richard III

Timeline

1485	Battle of Bosworth, Henry VII defeats Richard III ending Yorkist rule
1486	Lovel and Stafford Rebellion
1486–87	Simnel Rebellion
1487	Statute to limit the number of retainers
1489	Yorkshire Rebellion, Henry VII re-establishes Council of the North
1497	Cornish Rebellion
1497	Defeat of Perkin Warbeck
1504	Further statute to limit the number of retainers
1509	Accession of Henry VIII following death of Henry VII
1525	Unrest caused by the Amicable Grant
1529–30	Fall from power and death of Cardinal Thomas Wolsey
1529–36	Reformation of Parliament
1534	Act of Supremacy, Henry VIII made Head of the Church in England
1534–37	Silken Thomas Rebellion in Ireland
1536	Closure of the smaller monasteries, Lincolnshire Rising and Pilgrimage of Grace
1537	Bigod's Rising
1538	Injunctions reinforce government attack on saints, pilgrimages and holy days
1539	Act of Six Articles, gives support to more conservative religious practices
1540	Execution of Thomas Cromwell, Henry VIII's chief minister
1543	Act for the Advancement of True Religion limits access to the Bible
1547	Death of Henry VIII, Lord Protector Somerset rules on behalf of Edward VI. Dissolution of the chantries
1548	Establishment of Enclosure Commission. Unrest at Northaw, Hertfordshire and Helston, Cornwall
1549	Introduction of new Prayer Book, Western and Kett's Rebellions, unrest in much of southern and central England. Introduction of Lord Lieutenants
1549–50	Overthrow of Duke of Somerset as Lord Protector; replaced by Duke of Northumberland
1552	Execution of Duke of Somerset. Rigorous enforcement of anti-enclosure legislation, revaluation of coinage to halt inflation, arable farming protected and new Poor Law introduced
1553	Death of Edward VI and attempt by Duke of Northumberland to place Lady Jane Grey on the throne fails. Mary Tudor accedes to the throne, Northumberland executed
1554	Wyatt's Rebellion. Mary marries Philip of Spain
1558	Death of Mary Tudor, Elizabeth I inherits. Militia Acts
1558–67	Shane O'Neill unrest in Ireland
1559	Elizabethan Religious Settlement
1563	Statute of Artificers
1568	Arrival of Mary Queen of Scots in England
1569–70	Plot to marry Mary to Duke of Norfolk, rebellion of the Northern Earls
1569–73	Munster or Fitzgerald Rebellion
1570	Papal bull excommunicates Elizabeth
1571	Penal laws introduced against Catholic recusants
1572	Council of the North reformed, Poor Law Act
1579–83	Geraldine Rebellion
1583	Throckmorton Plot
1586	Book of Orders gives advice to JPs on how to deal with food shortages
1587	Execution of Mary Queen of Scots
1588	Defeat of Spanish Armada
1592–93	Statute Regarding the Export of Corn
1595–1603	Tyrone's Rebellion
1596	Oxfordshire Rising
1598	Statute against the Conversion to Pasture, Statute against the Engrossing of Farms
1601	Essex Rebellion

Answers

Page 7, Develop the detail

Dynastic rebellions were a cause of unrest throughout the period to a limited extent. This was because the Tudor regime became more secure as the period progressed. There was a lot of dynastic unrest at the start of the period **with challenges from the Yorkists and Pretenders**. The reign of Henry VII saw the most dynastic unrest as there were attempts to remove the Tudors, **with attempts from Lovel and Stafford, and also Simnel and Warbeck,** but there was also dynastic unrest under the later Tudor rulers, **with Northumberland's attempt to prevent Mary's accession,** although the challenge was not as serious. There were also attempts to alter the succession, although not necessarily to remove the Tudors, **as happened with the Pilgrim's attempt to restore Mary to the succession.**

Page 9, Turning assertion into argument

Dynastic problems were a major cause of unrest during the reign of Henry VII because **of Henry VII's weak claim to the throne and the survival of a number of Yorkists with stronger claims.**

However, their importance declined as the period progressed because **the Tudors were able to remove the Yorkists.**

Although dynastic issues were still a cause of unrest in Elizabeth I's reign as **she was seen as illegitimate by some Catholics who wanted Mary Queen of Scots to rule.**

Page 11, Spot the mistake

The paragraph deals only with the Yorkshire Rebellion. There is no comparison with other taxation rebellions and therefore, even if there is an argument, it cannot get beyond Level IB. The answer needs to compare the Yorkshire Rebellion with the Cornwall Rebellion and the Amicable Grant Rising to show evidence of continuity.

Page 13, Develop the detail

Religion was a cause of rebellion only during the middle part of the period, **from 1536 to 1569**. It was only when Henry VIII introduced religious changes, **such as the dissolution of the monasteries,** that it became a cause of unrest as before then the country was religiously united.

Religion was a particularly important cause of the Pilgrimage of Grace under Henry VIII, **as the rebels complained about the closure of the smaller monasteries and the loss of holy days,** although there were other causes of this rebellion, **such as taxation,** as well. It continued to be an important cause of rebellion under Edward VI, most notably in the Western Rebellion, where the rebels wanted to reverse the changes he had introduced, **particularly the introduction of a Protestant Prayer Book**. However, it was also a minor cause of Kett's Rebellion, where the rebels complained about the clergy **and their quality**. The last rebellion where religion was important was the rebellion of the Northern Earls, who had similar religious symbols as the Pilgrims, **such as the banner of the Five Wounds of Christ,** and restored traditional practices, **with the mass being said in Durham Cathedral**. However, after this rebellion religion played no further role in causing unrest, unlike other factors which remained a cause throughout the period.

Page 15, Developing an argument

Factional unrest affected every Tudor monarch. Henry VII faced challenges from the Yorkist faction following his victory at Bosworth. Simnel and his 3000 mercenaries fought Henry at Stoke and there was further factional conflict with Warbeck and Lovel and Stafford. **However, although these rebellions sometimes led to battle, the number of rebels was often small and therefore presented a limited threat.** There were also taxation rebellions in Yorkshire and Cornwall, **which attracted considerable support**. These rebellions forced the government to abandon the taxes. **Factional unrest continued** under Henry VIII; **however faction had become a subsidiary issue as** the large-scale rising against the Amicable Grant **was mainly aimed at the** prevention of further taxes, but it also attacked the king's chief minister, Wolsey. The 40,000 who rose in the Pilgrimage of Grace were mostly concerned by religious changes but also attacked Cromwell and attempted to restore the influence of Catherine of Aragon's supporters. **Similarly, the factional unrest later in the period attracted limited support;** Wyatt's Rebellion, which attracted 5000, was a response to the Spanish marriage and fears that courtiers would lose their positions. During Elizabeth's reign the Northern Earls rose with 5000 men, but fled when royal forces approached. Essex raised a few hundred men in his protest against his loss of influence. The city of London did not rise to support him. **Therefore, although factional unrest continued throughout the period, it did not attract large-scale support and at times was often only a subsidiary cause of unrest.**

Page 19, Identify an argument

Sample 1 contains the argument.

Page 19, Turning assertion into argument

Enclosure was a significant cause of social and economic unrest because it led to **widespread unrest across many counties as in 1549.**

However, in many social and economic rebellions enclosure was often just the trigger because **there were underlying causes such as the rise in prices or exploitation by the landlord.**

Also, enclosure unrest often failed to raise large numbers because **they were often protests in response into localised events, as with the Oxfordshire Rising in 1596.**

Page 23, Complete the paragraph

Rebellions in the period seldom had just one cause. This is seen most clearly in rebellion such as the Pilgrimage of Grace and Western Rebellion. Both rebellions had religion as their main cause, with the Pilgrims demanding the restoration of smaller monasteries and the Western demanding the abolition of the new Prayer Book. Both rebellions also wanted to protect traditional practices, such as holy days and the use of holy bread and water. The rebellions also had religious symbols as both marched under the banner of the Five Wounds of Christ. However, the rebels also had social and economic grievances about taxation, with the Pilgrims complaining about the Subsidy Act and the Western rebels about the Sheep Tax. **Even rebellions that appear to be dominated by one cause, such as religion, had secondary causes, such as social and economic grievances, which helped to swell the rebel ranks.**

Section 2: The frequency and nature of disturbances

Page 25, Develop the detail

Many rebellions throughout the period attempted to seize regional capitals**, such as York, Exeter or Norwich**. Regional capitals were administrative centres and their seizure presented a direct challenge to the government which would have to send in troops to regain control as happened in 1549 **when Norwich was taken by Kett**. Regional capitals were often the seats of the local bishops and in

religious protests the rebels wanted to control these **as happened in both 1536 with York and 1569 with Durham**. However, they were not always successful in taking them, even when they laid siege to them **as happened with Exeter in 1549**. It was not just regional capitals that the rebels attempted to seize. Many rebellions, **such as Wyatt's and Essex,** attempted to take the capital city itself because it was the centre of government. The situation in Ireland was very different as the rebel tactics were not the same and the seizure of major towns or cities did not occur.

Page 27, Delete as applicable

To a **fair** extent 1549 was the most important turning point in the nature of Tudor rebellions from 1485 to 1603. **Some** rebellions in the period before 1549 lasted a few months. This was particularly noticeable with the Pilgrimage of Grace which lasted two months and was similar to the major disturbances of Kett's and the Western Rebellion in 1549. The Oxfordshire Rising of 1596 and Essex Rebellion in 1601 were **much shorter** in length. However, Irish rebellions which became more frequent in the period after 1549 **challenge** this view as they sometimes lasted for a number of years. In this way, to a **fair** extent 1549 was the most important turning point in the nature of Tudor rebellions from 1485 to 1603 because **in England the duration of rebellions generally declined, but this was not the case in Ireland.**

Page 27, Turning assertion into argument

During the first half of the period the Tudor monarchy had been challenged by the Yorkists, but in the second half of the period this threat had been removed because **most of the Yorkists had been killed.**

During the period after 1536 religious changes had caused unrest but after 1559 this declined because **of the moderate nature of Elizabeth's Religious Settlement**.

Also, the increased use of Parliament meant that unrest was reduced because **legislation was passed that dealt with many of the causes of social and economic disquiet.**

Page 29, Complete the paragraph

Although many nobles were more reluctant to engage in rebellion, there were those for whom rebellion was their only way of restoring their position and economic fortune. This point is supported by the fact that during the reign of Elizabeth individual nobles such as Westmorland, Northumberland and Essex led rebellions against the monarch. These nobles felt they were losing power had little to lose; the Northern Earls had lost control of the wardenships of the Marches and Essex had lost his monopoly over sweet wine. Although they were able to attract support from some other nobles such as Southampton and Rutland, they were not able to attract popular support, with the Northern Earls raising only 5000 men. In comparison, the government was able to rely on the support of most of the nobility. In the rebellion of the Northern Earls, Hunsdon, Huntingdon and Sussex were able to raise troops, which forced the Northern Earls to flee, and this can be contrasted with the Pilgrimage of Grace earlier in the period. Although there was something of a change in the number of nobles involved in rebellion and the scale of those risings, the later period still witnessed noble unrest.

Page 31, Identify an argument

Sample 2 contains the argument.

Page 33, Spot the mistake

There is no synthesis within the paragraph, although two religiously motivated rebellions are mentioned they are not compared for similarity or difference.

Page 33, Eliminate irrelevance

Many Tudor rebellions wanted to reverse government policies. This was particularly true of religiously motivated rebellions where the rebels wanted to stop religious innovation, such as in the Pilgrimage of Grace where they wanted to preserve traditional religious institutions, such as monasteries. Monasteries were often the places where local people worshipped or provided employment, therefore the rebels restored some of the smaller monasteries in Lancashire. This was similar in the Western Rebellion which was caused by the introduction of the new Prayer Book. ~~There had been religious tensions in Cornwall before this and therefore further religious protest was not surprising~~. Similarly, the rebels in the rebellion of the Northern Earls were concerned by the establishment of a Protestant regime in the North, ~~but they also drew up a plan to marry the Duke of Norfolk to Mary Queen of Scots~~. However, in contrast, Kett's rebels wanted to increase the moves of Somerset's government towards Protestantism and wanted the government to ensure priests were resident and could teach the people.

Page 35, Delete as applicable

Some Tudor rebellions were badly organised. For example, the leadership of the rebellion of the Northern Earls was similar to that of all rebellions to a **fair** extent in that it lacked commitment from

the rebels and was poorly informed. In contrast, Aske was similar to **some** of the other rebel leaders in ensuring that the Pilgrim rebels did not disperse and that order was maintained within the forces monarchs were concerned to bring in men whom they could trust, **Elizabeth brought in the Earl of Huntingdon who had no connections with the area,** and remove those who were less reliable, **particularly Catholic JPs,** even if they had not been involved in unrest, and this was done in a number of areas of local government. This often meant that men of a lower social status, who owed their power to the monarch, were brought in, **most notably under Henry VIII as deputy wardens,** to replace those who had influence in the area. Some monarchs went even further and visited the North, **as Henry VIII did after the Pilgrimage of Grace,** but this was not a regular occurrence.

Section 3: The impact of disturbances on Tudor governments

Page 43, Develop the detail

When the government discovered that there was trouble, talks were often held between the monarch and councillors to decide what action to take and this could delay their response to the unrest. Henry VII consulted his trusted **household** servants or called a meeting of nobles **in a Great Council** to decide what to do **about the invasion of Simnel**; this was different to Elizabeth and Mary **who relied on secretaries and councillors to devise strategy**. However, Henry VIII also left similar problems for his ministers, **such as Wolsey and Cromwell,** to deal with. Somerset on the other hand adopted a different approach **and failed to consult his councillors**. Consultation and information gathering were lengthy processes, as the government wanted to know all the details about the unrest in order to decide what action to take. There were often delays in gathering information and this made the government appear slow.

Page 43, Turning assertion into argument

Some Tudor governments had problems gathering information because **communication with peripheral regions was slow**.

However, Henry VII's use of spies was successful because **he had spies in European courts**.

Also, the significant use of spies under Elizabeth helped as it **kept her informed of the movements of Mary Queen of Scots and led to a decline in unrest.**

Page 49, Delete as applicable

It is **correct** to state that not all rebellions ended in battle. Dynastic rebellions often ended in battle as the rebels had to defeat the monarch in order to take the throne as was seen with the Simnel Rebellion where over 4000 of Simnel's mercenaries were killed. Popular rebellions were also **more likely** to end in battle. This view is also **incorrect** for Irish rebellions. Similarly, as the period progressed it was **less likely** for rebellion to end in battle. Consequently, it is **correct** to state that not all rebellion ended in battle because **the government wanted to avoid battles if possible**.

Page 49, Identify an argument

Sample 1 contains the argument.

Page 51, Complete the paragraph

Henry VII's treatment of rebels was similar to that of Mary Tudor. Although rebels who engaged in treasonous activities knew that the penalty was death, not all rebels were put to death. As a consequence some potential rebels had bonds and recognisances imposed upon them. Mary Tudor was also lenient in her treatment of rebels after Wyatt's Rebellion, pardoning over 600 following his rebellion. However, Henry VIII, Edward VI and Elizabeth I were harsh in their treatment of rebels. After both the Pilgrimage of Grace in 1536–37 and the Western Rebellion of 1549 over 100 rebels were put to death, but after the rebellion of the Northern Earls in 1569 over 450 rebels were hanged and even after the minor Oxfordshire Rising of 1596, Elizabeth put all four ringleaders to death. It would therefore be fair to conclude that **some monarchs were harsh in their treatment of rebels, with Henry VIII and Elizabeth being particularly harsh, whereas Henry VII and Mary were more lenient**.

Page 53, Spot the mistake

The answer considers only developments in the reign of Henry VII, but as this is a synoptic paper examples must be drawn from across the period and comparisons made.

Page 55, Develop the detail

Perhaps the most notable area where royal authority was strengthened in response to rebellion was in the peripheral counties of the North. The North was a dangerous area for the Tudors. This was clearly seen in the reigns of both Henry VIII and Elizabeth I who took action to improve royal control **by reforming the Council of the North** after the Pilgrimage of Grace and the rebellion of the Northern Earls. The period. Henry VII was to a **fair** extent reliant upon his nobility for the maintenance of stability. The nobility were **very** important in putting down unrest as was seen by both the Simnel and Cornwall Rebellions. This pattern **stayed the same** under Henry VIII when dealing with the Pilgrimage of Grace where nobles such as **Norfolk** were important in negotiating with the rebels. During the reign of Edward and Elizabeth the role of the nobility in putting down disorder **stayed the same** with the use of Russell in 1549 and **Sussex** in 1569. However, the nobility were also a cause of unrest as seen most noticeably in the reigns of **Henry VII and Elizabeth** when they led rebellions. Overall, to a **fair** extent, the importance of the nobility changed in the maintenance of stability in the period because **they became involved in rebellions only when they were desperate and were more likely to be involved in their suppression**.

Page 57, Turning assertion into argument

Rebellions were a threat to Tudor governments in so far as some rebellions were able to **raise large numbers and attract foreign support**.

However, it was dynastic rebellions that were the greatest threat because **their ultimate aim was the removal of the monarch**.

Moreover, foreign support made these challenges greater because **mercenaries or trained soldiers were supplied by the foreign powers**.

Section 4: The maintenance of political stability

Page 59, Identify an argument

Sample 2 contains the argument.

Page 59, Turning assertion into argument

The institution of the monarchy was important in the maintenance of political stability because **the monarchs had ultimate authority as they were appointed by God and any rebellion against them was a sin**.

Moreover, monarchs worked hard to enhance their respect and aura because **they relied on patronage and rewards to maintain support**.

However, they were also dependent upon the support of the nobility because **the nobles were able to raise forces to help put down unrest**.

Page 61, Develop the detail

The Church was an important institution in the maintenance of stability. At every coronation monarchs were anointed with holy oil, a clear sign of the link between the Church and state. This link continued as many Tudor monarchs used bishops as administrators and for advice; **Henry VII used Fox and Warham, whilst Henry VIII used Cuthbert Tunstall**. Some monarchs appointed bishops to very high office, **with Henry VIII using Rowland Lee to run the Council of Wales,** a clear sign of their dependence on them in the government of the kingdom. This process continued for much of the period, although the second half of the period saw less use made of bishops as administrators. The Church was also able to support the monarch by threatening or actually excommunicating any who fought against the king **at the Battle of Stoke or those involved in Simnel's invasion or the Cornish fight at Blackheath**.

Page 65, Spot the mistake

The paragraph contains no synthesis. The answer does draw examples from two different rulers, but no comparison of similarity or difference is made, which is essential for Level II.

Page 69, Complete the paragraph

The nobility were important in maintaining stability in the peripheral regions of the country, particularly the North. Some families, such as the Percys, owned large amounts of land and were therefore able to rule as petty kings. They were able to raise considerable forces made up of their tenants, making them indispensable in the maintenance of order. Successive monarchs sought to bring such families under control through acts against livery and maintenance or by appointing local gentry, who owed their office to the Crown, to key jobs. As Lord Lieutenants or as presidents of regional councils the nobility were vital, acting as the principal upholder of order. **The nobility were therefore important throughout the period in the maintenance of stability in the peripheral areas, whether in raising troops to keep order or ensuring that disorder did not develop.**

Page 69, Delete as applicable

To a **limited** extent, the importance of the nobility changed in the maintenance of stability in the assembled. In Kett's Rebellion he was able to exert a **considerable** degree of control through the issuing of warrants. In conclusion, the examples of the Northern Earls, Aske and Kett show that organisation of Tudor rebellions was **sometimes** poor in the sense that **whilst some were poorly organised others were very well organised and controlled.**

Page 73, Turning assertion into argument

Respect for authority was important to Tudor governments because **they did not have a standing army or police force.**

Changing attitudes to disorder were also essential in maintaining stability because **they encouraged people to use litigation rather than disorder to settle disputes.**

Moreover, the gulf between the rich and poor helped maintain stability because **the wealthy realised they had less in common with the poor and therefore had more to gain in upholding order rather than leading riots.**